ZOROASTRIANISM
WORLD RELIGIONS

by
Paula R. Hartz

☑® Facts On File, Inc.

ZOROASTRIANISM, Updated Edition

World Religions

Facts On File, Inc.
132 West 31st Street
New York NY 10001

Library of Congress Cataloging-in-Publication Data

Hartz, Paula.
    Zoroastrianism / by Paula R. Hartz.—Updated ed.
        p. cm.— (World religions)
    Includes bibliographical references and index.
    ISBN 0-8160-5723-0 (alk. paper)
    1. Zoroastrianism—Juvenile literature. I. Title. II. Series.
BL1572.H37 2004
295—dc22   2004043346

Facts On File books are available at special discounts when purchased in bulk quantities for businesses, associations, institutions, or sales promotions. Please call our Special Sales Department in New York at 212/967-8800 or 800/322-8755.

You can find Facts On File on the World Wide Web at http://www.factsonfile.com

Developed by Brown Publishing Network, Inc.

Photo Research by Susan Van Etten

The author wishes to acknowledge the following for their encouragement and support: Professor Kaikhosrov D. Irani; Dr. Lovji Cama; Roshan Rivetna, editor, *FEZANA Journal;* the members of the Zoroastrian Association of New York (ZAGNY)

Photo credits:

Cover: Two winged sphinxes topped by a winged disk, emblem of the god Ahura Mazda. Enamelled brick panel from Susa, Iran. Achaemenid period, 6th-5th century B.C.E. © Erich Lessing/Art Resource, NY; Title page: Dastur Dr. Kaikhusroo M. JamaspaAsa performs a Navjote, or initiation, of a young American Zoroastrian, in Bombay, India, while family members watch and record the occasion for their family history. The initiation into the responsibilities of the religion consists of the first occasion when the child receives the sacred shirt and cord, *sudreh* and *kusti*, and says the *kusti* prayers as a public declaration of commitment. Prof. John R. Hinnells; Table of Contents page: Aerial view of the ruins of Persepolis, the palace built by the Persian emperor Darius I. Giraudon/Art Resource, NY; *Pages 6-7* Kaveh Kazermi/Panos Pictures; *8* Charles Lenars/Corbis; *15* Roger Wood/Corbis; *16* Roshan Rivetna, publisher of *FEZANA Journal;* *20-21* Christine Osborne/Middle East Pictures; *23* Courtesy of *FEZANA Journal;* *24* Christine Osborne/Middle East Pictures; *32-33* Patrick Syder/Middle East Pictures; *36* Scala/Art Resource, NY; *41* Roger Wood/Corbis; *46* Corbis/Bettmann-UPI; *48-49* Christine Osborne/Middle East Pictures; *52, 56* Prof. John R. Hinnels; *59, 60* Corbis/Reuters; *62* Kaveh Kazermi/Panos Pictures; *70* The Bodleian Library, University of Oxford. MS Zend. c.1, folio 192; *78-79* Prof. John R. Hinnells; *82, 84* Kaveh Kazermi/Panos Pictures; *87, 90-91* Prof. John R. Hinnells; *94, 97, 102* Kaveh Kazermi/Panos Pictures; *108-9* © Lindsay Hebberd/CORBIS; *111* Cyrus Rivetna, courtesy *FEZANA Journal;* *114,* Photo by Cyrus Rivetna, courtesy *The Legacy of Zarathushtra,* Ed. Roshan Rivetna, FEZANA, 2002; *120* Courtesy of *FEZANA Journal.*

Printed in the United States of America

VB PKG 10 9 8 7 6 5 4 3 2 1

This book is printed on acid-free paper.

TABLE OF CONTENTS

Preface   **4**

CHAPTER 1   **Introduction: The Good Religion of Zarathushtra**   **6**

CHAPTER 2   **Zarathushtra, Father of Zoroastrianism**   **20**

CHAPTER 3   **Zoroastrianism Through History**   **32**

CHAPTER 4   **Zoroastrianism in India: The Parsis**   **48**

CHAPTER 5   **The Avesta: The Zoroastrian Scripture**   **62**

CHAPTER 6   **Philosophy and Ethics in Zoroastrianism**   **78**

CHAPTER 7   **Rituals and Rites of Passage**   **90**

CHAPTER 8   **Zoroastrianism Facing the Future**   **108**

Glossary   **121**

Chapter Notes   **125**

For Further Reading   **125**

Index   **126**

Preface

We live in what is sometimes described as a "secular age," meaning, in effect, that religion is not an especially important issue for most people. But there is much evidence to the contrary. In many societies, including the United States, religion and religious values shape the lives of millions of individuals and play a key role in politics and culture as well.

The World Religions series, of which this book is a part, is designed to appeal to both students and general readers. The books offer clear, accessible overviews of the major religious traditions and institutions of our time. Each volume in the series describes where a particular religion is practiced, its origins and history, its central beliefs and important rituals, and its contributions to world civilization. Carefully chosen photographs complement the text, and a glossary and bibliography are included to help readers gain a more complete understanding of the subject at hand.

Religious institutions and spirituality have always played a central role in world history. These books will help clarify what religion is all about and reveal both the similarities and differences in the great spiritual traditions practiced around the world today.

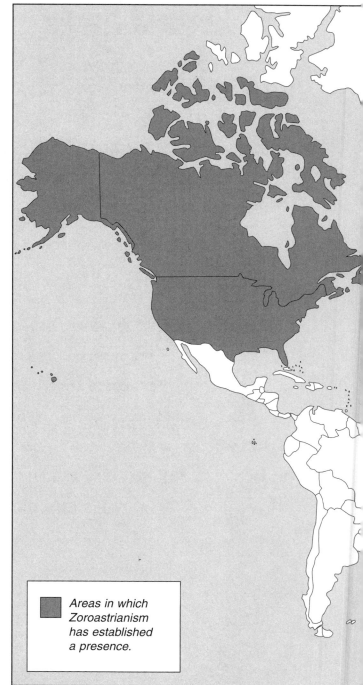

Areas in which Zoroastrianism has established a presence.

CHAPTER 1

Introduction: The Good Religion of Zarathushtra

Zoroastrianism has often been called the "Good Religion," because of its emphasis on goodness and on righteous thought and behavior. One of the oldest world religions, it arose in ancient Persia perhaps thirty-five hundred years ago. At that time, the prophet Zarathushtra—Zoroaster, as the Greeks called him—began preaching his message. Zarathushtra, who was apparently a priest of the existing Iranian religion of his time, was a highly original thinker and a bold reformer. His teachings may seem straightforward today, but in his time they were truly revolutionary.

Zarathushtra rejected many of the beliefs and practices of the existing religion. In a time of many gods, he preached about one great and supreme God, *Ahura Mazda*. In a time when most people believed that worship consisted mainly of elaborate rituals to satisfy angry deities, he preached a religion of personal ethics, in which people's actions in life were more important than ritual and sacrifice. Zarathushtra's preaching formed the basis of one of the most influential and long-lasting religions the world has ever known. His message is preserved in the *Avesta*, the Zoroastrian scripture.

The Zoroastrian Community

Zoroastrianism is the smallest of today's world religions. No one knows exactly how many people currently practice Zoroastrianism, but by most estimates it is about 150,000. This is a tiny minority compared to world religions such as Christianity and Islam, both of which have more than one billion followers. Yet Zoroastrians, or, as many of them prefer to be called, Zarathushtis, are a proud and active group, working hard to keep their religion alive and strong.

Zoroastrians are scattered all over the world. In Iran, the land where Zoroastrianism was born, only a small remnant of Zoroastrians remains. No one knows for certain how many Iranian Zoroastrians, or *Zartoshtis,* there are. Estimates range from fewer than 10,000 to 90,000, with most sources suggesting between 20,000 and 35,000. The largest concentration of Zoroastrians by far, about 100,000, live in India, where they are known as *Parsis,* a name that reflects their Persian heritage. Another 7,000 to 8,000 live in India's neighbor, Pakistan.

■ *A relief sculpture of the Zoroastrian symbol, or Faravahar, decorates a wall in the ruins of Persepolis.*

Zarathushtis have established themselves in many countries. There are formally organized Zarathushti federations in Australia and New Zealand, in England, in Singapore, in Germany, and in Scandinavia, among other places. North America has about 10,000 to 20,000 Zoroastrian followers who belong to Zarathushti organizations—in Boston, New York, Chicago, Houston, California, Washington State, Arizona, and Toronto.

The Basic Principles of Zoroastrianism

Zarathushtra revealed his vision of the good religion in a series of psalms, or *Gathas*. The Gathas are personal expressions of Zarathushtra's belief in Ahura Mazda and conversations with him. All Zoroastrian beliefs and rituals are based on them.

One God—Zarathushtra preached the existence of one supreme God, whose name, Ahura Mazda, means "Wise Lord." Ahura Mazda is the creator of the universe and all things in it, including humankind. Zarathushtra taught that Ahura Mazda is all-good and all-wise. He is the father of truth and goodness. He brings love and happiness, and is to be loved and respected, never feared.

The Twin Spirits: Truth and the Lie—According to Zarathushti belief, Ahura Mazda first created consciousness and a knowledge of perfect good, which is the Spirit of Truth, or *Spenta Mainyu*. But when he created the physical, or *Getig*, world, evil came into being in the form of ignorance, sin, and violation of the natural order. Zarathushtra called this Spirit of Evil, "The Lie," which later came to be called *Angra Mainyu* or *Ahriman*. The struggle between these opposing forces, which never agree, governs all human thought and activity.

Free Will—Ahura Mazda does not order every aspect of human life. At the time of creation he gave humanity the gift of free will. As Zarathushtis, men and women must think and reason for themselves. They have the freedom to choose good over evil. Free will and intellect give them the choice to do the will of Ahura Mazda—to live according to the Truth.

■ *Invocation of Asha (Righteousness)*

Most Zoroastrian devotions end with this prayer in Avestan. It is one of the three cardinal Zoroastrian prayers. It is spoken to concentrate the mind on "asha," or righteousness. It has many translations.

> Ashem vohu vahishtem asti, ushta asti, ushta ahmai,
>   hyat ashai, vahishtai ashem.

Asha is good, it is best. It is happiness. Happiness comes to the person who is righteous for the sake of utmost righteousness. (Ys. 28.1)
—*Daily Prayers of the Zoroastrians*, Framroz Rustomjee, 1959

The Creed of Zoroastrianism

The goal of those who follow *Zarathushti Din*—the Zoroastrian religion—is to live the truth according to the principles of Ahura Mazda. Zarathushtra rejected the idea that ritual was the way to reach out to Ahura Mazda. Religion, he taught, was within the individual. Each person is called upon to live according to a simple creed:

- Good Thoughts—*Humata*
- Good Words—*Hukhta*
- Good Deeds—*Huvarshta*

The most important goal of a Zarathushti is to have "Good Thoughts"—He attempts to imitate the Good Mind, or *Vohu Mana*, one of the highest attributes of Ahura Mazda. If a person has the good mind of Zoroastrianism, he or she will speak and do good, live well, and spread happiness in the world.

Zoroastrianism is a happy and optimistic religion. Pessimism and despair are considered sins—they represent giving in to evil. Zarathushtis are taught to love life and to enjoy life's pleasures. They are encouraged to work hard, to strive for excellence, to marry and raise families, and to be active members of the community. Enjoying festivals and social life is part of their philosophy, as is the duty to support one another in times of trouble. Zarathushtis believe that when they fight society's ills, such as sickness, poverty, and ignorance, they are working together with Ahura Mazda toward creating a perfect world. They do not practice self-denial and asceticism—that is, suffering for the sake of religious purity. In Zoroastrianism, to withdraw from the world is considered sinful. Instead Zarathushtis live fully in the world, enjoying all the good things in their earthly life.

The Amesha Spentas

In the battle between Truth and the Lie, Ahura Mazda is assisted by the *Amesha Spentas,* or Benevolent Spirits, which are aspects of his own power. The Amesha Spentas are sometimes represented as angelic beings, but in the spiritual sense they are sparks of the divine that every person may cultivate within himself or herself. The highest ideal for humankind is to live these ideals. There are six Amesha Spentas:

- *Vohu Mana*, the spirit of the Good Mind. From the Good Mind comes Good Thoughts, and from Good Thoughts follow Good Words and Good Deeds. To live according to Zoroastrianism, people must strive constantly to cultivate the Good Mind within themselves, enabling them to grasp Asha. It is Vohu Mana that enables people to recognize good and evil in their lives.

- *Asha Vahista,* the spirit of Truth and Righteousness. Asha (pronounced ah SHAH) embodies righteousness, truth, wisdom, justice, and progress. The path of Asha leads to salvation and blessing. To follow it is the highest ideal of Zoroastrianism—being righteous.
- *Khshathra Vairya,* the spirit of Ideal Authority or Dominion. This spirit is the power of Ahura Mazda as a wise ruler. The spirit of strength and authority comes in this life to those who have the Good Mind and follow the path of Asha. In this spirit, humans promote good and fight evil in the world.
- *Spenta Armaity,* the spirit of Love and Benevolence. It is Armaity that motivates people to love humankind. Through Spenta Armaity come charity and grace.
- *Haurvatat,* the spirit of Perfection and Well-being in this life.
- *Ameratat,* the spirit of Immortality and eternal bliss.

Ahura Mazda is all-powerful, but he does not control human actions. When he gave people free will, he made them responsible for their own lives and behavior. To take away free will after once giving it would be wrong. Free will and intellect offer humans the choice to do the will of Ahura Mazda—to live according to the Truth.

The Fravashis

To help people choose the truth, each person is born with a *fravashi,* a guardian spirit that helps him or her tell good from evil, right from wrong. People may recognize their own fravashi when it guides their conscience. It is more than conscience, however, because a conscience must be developed as a person grows, but the fravashi is inborn. Fravashis are spiritual beings that existed before the physical world was created. They are born into this world with each new life and remain with an individual until death. Then they leave to return to the company of other fravashis, remaining, however, a link between the living and the dead. They may be ritually called upon to communicate with the soul of the dead person. The fravashi is the spark of the divine essence of Ahura Mazda that is in all living things.

The Restoration of the World

Zoroastrians believe that the battle between Ahura Mazda, the perfect good, and Angra Mainyu, the evil spirit, will go on for thousands of years. At the end of time, a Savior, or *Sashoyant*, will lead people successfully and definitively against the forces of evil and ignorance. There will be a mighty battle between Ahura Mazda and Angra Mainyu. The world will be destroyed by fire. Molten metal will cover the earth like water. The righteous will wade through, but the unrighteous will be consumed by it. Evil, sin, and death will be defeated. The world will be purified and perfected.

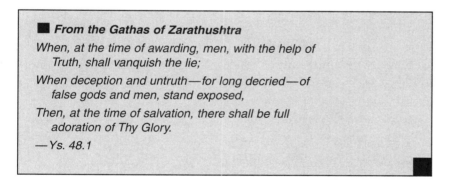

■ *From the Gathas of Zarathushtra*

When, at the time of awarding, men, with the help of Truth, shall vanquish the lie;

When deception and untruth—for long decried—of false gods and men, stand exposed,

Then, at the time of salvation, there shall be full adoration of Thy Glory.

—Ys. 48.1

In the renewal of the world, all the dead will rise. The gates of hell will open, and those souls, too, will rise, purified and redeemed. People will live together in harmony in the perfect world of Ahura Mazda for all eternity. This time it is called *Frashogard*, or *Frashokereti*, which means "renewal."

All Zarathushtis have a duty to fight constantly against the weaknesses within the human heart and the worldly temptations that form the Lie. The forces of good, which Ahura Mazda leads, are engaged in a continual struggle with the forces of evil. In choosing good, Zarathushtis join with Ahura Mazda to help bring about a perfect world.

The Importance of Doing Good

Zarathushtra urged his followers to care for and defend the poor. Since the very beginning of the religion, service to others has been a tenet of Zoroastrianism. Every Zarathushti is expected to share happiness, which means sharing wealth, time, and talents freely and generously. For Zarathushtis, it is not enough just to think good thoughts and speak good words—one must actively work to combat evil and ignorance. In everything they do, they are asked to consider not only their own welfare, but the welfare of the community. This is the spirit of Armaity, which encourages people to reach out to others in goodness and charity.

Zoroastrians are known for supporting each other in both spiritual and practical ways. But they also contribute generously to worthy causes outside the Zoroastrian community. In India, where Zoroastrians have had a long presence, many schools, hospitals, and other worthwhile projects were founded with Zoroastrian time, energy, and financial assistance. In actively serving their communities, Zarathushtis are following their Prophet and living their religion.

Zoroastrian Worship

Zoroastrianism is not a congregational religion. It has rich and meaningful rituals, which priests perform on a regular daily basis in their largest and most sacred places of worship, but laypeople are not expected to attend. Zarathushtis gather mainly for the New Year, or *No Roz,* festival and the six major festivals, or *gahambars,* which occur throughout the year. On these occasions, they get together for prayers followed by a shared meal and cultural activities such as singing and dancing.

Otherwise, prayers are said individually or in family groups. The day is divided into five ritual periods, or *gahs.* They occur in the morning, midday, afternoon, evening, and at night.

The ruins of an ancient Zoroastrian fire temple stand on a hill near Isfahan, Iran. The dramatic setting suggests the importance placed on worship.

At each of these times, a Zarathushti pauses to repeat the appropriate prayer from the Avesta, the Zoroastrian scripture.

The Sacred Fire

For Zarathushtis, fire is the sacred symbol of Ahura Mazda. It captures the brilliance of the sun and the heavenly bodies, and it speaks of the power, might, and energy of Truth. In its purest form, it represents the highest truth. Priests conduct all religious rituals and ceremonies in the presence of fire, which signifies the presence of Ahura Mazda. The most sacred fires of Zoroastrianism are consecrated fires, which contain fire from sixteen different sources, ritually combined in a long series of purification rites. One part of a consecrated fire is fire caused by lightning, since it comes directly from Ahura Mazda.

■ *Mobeds conduct a ritual before an* afargan, *or fire urn, in the fire room of the Darbe-Mehr in Chicago. They wear white, the color of purity. Mouth veils prevent their breath from polluting the sacred fire.*

It is important to remember, however, that Zarathushtis do not worship fire. The sacred fire is not an object of worship in itself, but a symbol and reminder of Ahura Mazda, the Wise Lord and great God.

Sacred Places: Fire Temples

Fire temples house the sacred fires of Zoroastrianism. There are three grades of fire temples. These are *Atash Behram, Atash Adaran,* and *Atash Dadga.* An Atash Behram is the highest grade of temple. Sometimes referred to as a "fire cathedral," it houses the holiest of consecrated fires. The highest and most sacred of all Zoroastrian rituals are held there, conducted by the high priests of Zoroastrianism. There are only ten Atash Behrams in the world: eight in India and two in Iran.

Inside the fire temple is an entrance hall with a source of water so that people may bathe the exposed parts of their bodies before prayer. Like fire, water is a sacred creation of Ahura Mazda, and people offer prayers before it as well. At the center of the building is the "fire room." This room contains the *afargan,* a large urn that holds the fire. The fire is kept burning day and night. It is tended regularly by priests in a ceremony known as *Boi.* The fire room has no decorations. There are no statues and no pictures on the wall—nothing to detract from the beauty and power of the fire. In an Atash Behram, only fully initiated priests may enter the fire room. Properly initiated and ritually pure Zarathushti worshipers may, if they wish, observe the rites through iron bars or grillwork that separate them from the sacred fire.

In the rest of the fire temple are meeting rooms, lecture halls, and a library. These rooms, which have no sacred significance, may have portraits or plaques commemorating donors and paintings that represent the prophet Zarathushtra. The entrances to the building are often decorated with flowers and beadwork, signifying that the building is a place of happiness.

An Atash Adaran also houses consecrated fire. It differs from an Atash Behram in the number of rituals performed in establishing the temple and the number and type of ceremonies a priest must perform before entering the fire room.

The fire in an Atash Dadga is similar to a household fire. Although still worthy of reverence, it is not specially consecrated. In India, this grade of temple is known as an *agiary.* In North America, it is called a *Darbe Mehr* or *Dar-e Meher.* No high rituals are held there, and there may be no full-time priest. If the fire is kept burning at all times, it may be fed by a layperson who has bathed and put on clean clothes. Special ceremonies, such as weddings, funerals, and initiations are performed by priests who come for the occasion. These, too, are always performed in the presence of fire.

Zoroastrianism and Other Religions

Zoroastrianism has much in common with other world religions, several of which it influenced. Like religions such as Judaism, Christianity, and Islam, it is monotheistic—that is, its followers believe in one supreme God. They believe in life after death and in heaven and hell. Zoroastrianism also has a strong code of ethics that its believers are expected to follow in their daily lives. Like Christianity, Islam, and Buddhism, it had a specific founder who came to reform older religious practices. But it differs from other religions in significant ways. Unlike Islam, it is not fatalistic. The evil in the world is not the will of God, but exists because of flaws in the material world and within the human heart. Zoroastrians control their destiny after death by their actions on earth, their choice of good and truth over ignorance and evil.

Like Christians and Jews, Zoroastrians believe that a savior will come at the end of time, to lead the faithful into a perfected world. But Zoroastrianism differs from Christianity, whose believers are saved by faith in Jesus Christ and by God's grace rather than by their good works. Also, Zoroastrians do not believe in original sin. People are born pure, but may be influenced by the evil around them. For Zoroastrians, it is a lifetime of following the teachings of Zarathushtra that brings about salvation, not faith alone. Zoroastrianism also differs from Hinduism in that there is no belief in reincarnation and no transmigration of the soul. People live on this earth but once and have only one chance to find their way to eternal peace.

The Importance of Zoroastrianism

Zoroastrianism holds a unique place in the history of religion. Its founder and prophet, Zarathushtra, originated the concept of one great and supreme God. He proposed an explanation for the problem of evil in a world created by a good God, through the notion of the twin mentalities, Truth and the Lie, which are present in the human heart, and through the imperfection in the material world. Zoroastrianism thus answers the question with which all religions must struggle: "How can a good and loving God permit evil and suffering in the world?" Zoroastrians believe that evil and suffering are the work of the Lie, Angra Mainyu, and not of Ahura Mazda, who battles evil and sin and will eventually defeat it.

Zarathushtra also introduced the concept of an afterlife in which people would be welcomed into the glory of Ahura Mazda or dropped into the pit as a result of their actions on earth. In Angra Mainyu, Zoroastrianism gave the world the concept of Satan, the tempter and ruler of the underworld.

Zarathushtra spoke of a Savior who would come to lead the righteous at the end of the world, and of a final judgment in which the existing world would be destroyed and a new, perfect world would come into being. He offered humankind free will, with which to choose good over evil in order to perfect the world in a joint venture with Ahura Mazda. He changed the ancient Iranian polytheistic notion of religion as a way of attempting to calm angry gods to one of ethical actions on the part of humans. In the ancient Iranian society where women had lesser roles to play, he declared that they were religiously equal to men and also capable of salvation.

Zorastrianism is believed to have influenced other world religions with which it came into contact. Some see Cyrus, the Great King of Persia, who liberated the Jews in 537 B.C.E. from their captivity in Babylon, as one who brought the Zoroastrian monotheistic view of God to the Hebrew people and through them to Christianity. They also credit Cyrus with introducing the concept of a Messiah or Savior that flourished in the Jewish and Christian worlds. Zoroastrian teachings such as heaven and hell and final judgment also are viewed as having entered Islam when Muslim rulers took over Persia in the 7th century C.E.

Most of all, Zoroastrianism has proved to be a durable and lasting faith. Its followers, although few in number, are the proud keepers of a heritage that goes back thousands of years.

CHAPTER 2

Zarathushtra, Father of Zoroastrianism

*F*ew facts can be known about Zarathushtra, or Zoroaster, as the Greeks called him. We know that he was a real person, and that he lived in very ancient times. During his lifetime, the peoples of the Iranian Plateau, his homeland, kept no written documents, so we have no eyewitness accounts of his life. We do not even know for certain when he lived. The Greeks, who wrote of him first, knew only that the traditions concerning his life were already centuries old. They estimated that he had lived some six thousand years earlier than the philosopher Plato. Later historians reckoned that Zarathushtra had lived around 600 B.C.E., around the time of the Hebrew prophets. Today's scholars believe that Zarathushtra lived between 1500 and 1000 B.C.E. But even this is a wide range of time.

The earliest versions of Zarathushtra's life were passed down orally for more than a thousand years before they were recorded in writing, so it is hard to know how accurate they are. However, they provide some important clues to the man and his life. Our best knowledge of Zarathushtra comes from his own writings and his influence. One way scholars trace Zarathushtra's

life is by looking for clues in the Gathas, the ancient hymns that are believed to have been the work of Zarathushtra himself.

Zarathushtra's Words

Throughout his life, Zarathushtra composed hymns or psalms to the glory of Ahura Mazda. They are composed in Zarathushtra's language, *Gathic Avestan*. The Gathas are poems in complex metrical forms that were difficult to master. In Zarathushtra's time, such learning was largely confined to the priesthood, and his use of poetic form suggests that he had priestly training. The Gathas are of high literary quality. They show Zarathushtra to have been, not only a great religious thinker, but also one of Persia's earliest and finest poets.

Gathic Avestan, the language of the Gathas, is a very ancient dialect, one that was spoken only in a small area and for a relatively short time. This dialect provides important clues to Zarathushtra's origins.

■ Representations of Zarathushtra

Since he lived more than three thousand years ago, no one knows what Zarathushtra looked like. Artistic renderings of him, however, all look alike, even to the pose—a man gazing upward to the right, one hand raised. Until the eighteenth century, there were no portraits of Zarathushtra. Then a Zoroastrian artist had a dream in which the Prophet appeared to him. He painted the man he saw, and Zoroastrians since that time have accepted his vision as the way Zarathushtra looked.

Zarathushtra's Probable Origins

Although many areas of Iran have claimed him, Zarathushtra was probably born in what was then northeastern Persia, roughly where the boundaries of modern Iran, Afghanistan, and Turkmenistan meet today. Persia—which eventually stretched from the steppes of Russia and the Caspian Sea, westward to the Greek Empire, and south toward modern Pakistan—had not yet become an empire.

■ *A classic portrait of Zarathushtra in traditional Persian costume.*

From the Avesta, the Zoroastrian holy book, we know the names of Zarathushtra's mother, Dughda, and his father, Pourushasp, of the Spitama clan. Tradition has it that Zarathushtra was born in their home on the banks of the Daraja River. His followers celebrate his birthday on the sixth day of the first month, *Farvardin* (March–April) on the Zoroastrian calendar.

The Spitamas were a pastoral people who probably raised and traded horses. Zarathushtra himself, however, was apparently drawn to religion from an early age. The Gathas he composed suggest that he knew the religious traditions well and had been trained as a priest.

A village in northern Iran. Many people live much as they did in Zarathushtra's time, farming and raising sheep and goats.

Zarathushtra's Miraculous Beginnings

According to the later legendary Zoroastrian tradition, the coming of Zarathushtra was foretold long before his birth. The creatures of the earth and the saints of the heavens had spoken of it from the beginnings of the world. The heavenly glory that would pass to Zarathushtra came from the sun, moon, and stars into the home of Zarathushtra's mother, Dughda, even before her birth, starting an ever-burning fire on the hearth. When Dughda was born, she glowed with light. Evil powers tried to convince Dughda's father that the light around her showed she was a sorceress. He sent her away from his home, but in her new home she met Pourushasp, who was to be her husband.

As Dughda and Pourushasp were walking, Dughda saw and admired a plant. Pourushasp picked it for her and carried it home. It was a *haoma*, the sacred plant of Zoroastrian ritual. Inside was hidden Zarathushtra's guardian spirit, or *fravaha*, which would join him at birth. In this way, the divine spirit came into their home. Zarathushtra was born soon afterward, surrounded by light. As a newborn baby he laughed, and he spoke to Ahura Mazda, dedicating his life to the Wise Lord.

Zoroastrian legend says that evil spirits set out immediately to destroy this child that would conquer them. They persuaded Pourushasp that the radiant infant was a demon. The father laid his son on a pile of firewood and tried to light it, but the fire would not burn. Then he put the baby in the path of stampeding oxen, but the first ox stood over the baby and protected him. Zarathushtra was put into the den of a wolf whose cubs had been taken away, but instead of harming him, she cared for him. The theme of Zarathushtra's special relationship with animals recurs, underscoring his protection of them from animal sacrifice.

Zarathushtra survived other trials as a baby and child, always protected by his own essential goodness and righteousness.

The miraculous happenings surrounding Zarathushtra's birth tie elements of Zoroastrianism, such as the sacred fire and the haoma plant, to the life of the Prophet. These traditions glorify the life of a man of humble origins whose thought and philosophy were a turning point in religious history.

■ **The Birth of Zarathushtra, from the Denkard portion of the Avesta:**

"Further, when he [Zarathushtra] was born, there was a light like the blaze of fire, a glare and a twilight irradiating from his house in all directions, high in the air and to a great distance on the earth, as a token of his greatness and exaltation..."

—Denkard *Book 5, Chapter 2, Sanjana Edition*

The Zoroastrian Tradition

The Greeks first learned of Zoroaster and his message around 400 B.C.E. from the Magi, a priestly tribe of western Iran. By then, Zoroastrianism had had time to spread from the extreme eastern boundaries of Iran to the west. The Magi adopted Zoroastrian belief and claimed Zarathushtra as one of their own. They placed him as having lived some two hundred years earlier. Parts of the Avesta, the Zoroastrian scripture that was compiled over many centuries, gave the date of his birth as somewhere between 630 and 618 B.C.E., about a hundred years before the time of the Persian ruler Cyrus the Great.

When Zarathushtra was fifteen, according to the local custom, he was considered an adult. He put on the sacred sash of the existing Iranian religion, and took up adult duties. He apparently married and fathered a child. But he was restless. Born into violent times, he had seen much human suffering. Even at this young age, he had begun to consider the question of righteousness and the conflict between good and evil in the world. At twenty, over his parents' objections, he left home and began a period of wandering with his wife and young son, inquiring about the nature of righteousness.

Zarathushtra's Early Ministry

By the time Zarathushtra was thirty, he had become a priest. To participate in the spring festival, he went to the Daitya River, where one of his priestly duties was to go to the river at dawn to draw water from the deepest and purest part of the stream for the morning ceremony.

As he waded back to the riverbank, a glorious angel, Vohu Mana, stood before him. The angel asked him who he was and what was the most important thing in his life. Zarathushtra replied that he wanted most of all to be righteous and pure and to gain wisdom. With that, the angel took Zarathushtra into the presence of Ahura Mazda and the archangels. Zarathushtra tells of his vision in the Gathas:

> Then thus spake Ahura Mazda, the Lord of knowledge
> and wisdom:

"As there is not a righteous spiritual lord, or secular chief
So have I, indeed, the Creator, made thee, Zarathushtra, the leader,
For the welfare of the world and its diligent people."
    (Ys. 29.6)

Scarcely able to believe what he hears, Zarathushtra asks whom Ahura Mazda has chosen to carry his divine word and the welfare of the world. Ahura Mazda responds:

And thus spoke Ahura Mazda:
"The one who alone has harkened to my command and is known to me is Zarathushtra Spitama.
For his creator and for Truth, he wishes to announce the Holy Message,
Wherefore shall I bestow on him, the charm of speech."
    (Ys. 29.8)

In this way, Zarathushtra is ordained to be Ahura Mazda's prophet, and receives directly from him the gift of preaching.

Zarathushtra understood that he had received a special calling. He also understood that the way would be difficult, because it meant opposing the old religion and the princes who used it to their own ends. During the next few years, he often felt despair and called on Ahura Mazda to help him. He received other visions, seven in all, in which one by one all of the archangels, or Beneficent Immortals, appeared to him. These visions helped him to remain faithful to his work. For the next ten years, Zarathushtra preached his belief in the courts of the local rulers.

Zarathushtra's Message

Zarathushtra arose as a prophet who strongly denounced the ritual practices of the warrior societies, the groups of young men that wandered the countryside in a state of drunkenness, stealing and slaughtering cattle and terrorizing people. An outspoken reformer, Zarathushtra fought against the cruel and bloody practice of animal sacrifice, the use of intoxicating herbs, and the excesses of the old religion that whipped young men into a frenzy and sent them into battle. Never afraid to speak out, he openly scorned the "mumbling" priests and sacrificers. Instead of ritual, he demanded that people turn their hearts and minds to Ahura Mazda.

Zarathushtra preached the notion of one true god, Ahura Mazda, who had created human life and all things, visible and invisible. Along with all the things of the earth, two opposing forces were created. One force, Spenta Mainyu, the holy spirit, represented Truth and Goodness. The other, a destructive spirit that came to be called Angra Mainyu, represented the Lie. Zarathushtra saw a world of ethical good, in which people worked to maintain life by marrying, bringing up children, raising cattle, and farming. They would think good thoughts and do good deeds, turning away from evil and creating a peaceful, loving society. After death, people would be judged according to how they had chosen to live their lives. It was up to humans to choose Truth over the Lie.

Zarathushtra prophesied that the world would end in a final fire, in which all evil would be destroyed. The righteous would be saved. The gates of the underworld would be opened, and evildoers would be cleansed by the fires. They too would rise, and the whole world would be made perfect.

The ideas of one supreme God, the struggle between good and evil in the human soul, and a last judgment after death do not seem very unusual today, but in Zarathushtra's time they were revolutionary. Also revolutionary was his declaration that women, who held little or no place in society, were equal with men in the sight of Ahura Mazda and had the same hope of salvation.

Zarathushtra Wins Converts

For the first ten years of his mission, Zarathushtra traveled around, preaching in the courts of local rulers. His efforts were unsuccessful. At the age of forty, after ten years of preaching and teaching, Zarathushtra finally made his first convert. It was his cousin, Maidyoimanha, or Medyomah, the son of his father's brother. This was an important milestone, but Zarathushtra himself wondered whether the struggle was worthwhile—in ten years, he had won only one person to the side of Ahura Mazda.

Meanwhile, Zarathushtra's preaching had caused him many problems. He had angered the priests and teachers of the existing order. They denounced him and his message. Despairing, he turned to Ahura Mazda:

> *To what land shall I flee? Where bend my steps?*
> *I am thrust out from family and tribe:*
> *I have no favor from the village to which I would belong,*
> *Nor from the wicked rulers of the country.*
>   (Ushtavaiti Gatha, Ys. 46.1)

Zarathushtra fled. He took refuge in the court of Kai Vishtaspa, an Iranian ruler. At first he was not well received; for a time he languished in prison. As the story goes, Vishtaspa had

■ *Founders of World Religions*		
Abraham	*c. 1600–1300* B.C.E.	Judaism
Moses	*c. 1600–1300* B.C.E.	Judaism
Zarathushtra	*c. 1500–1000* B.C.E.	Zoroastrianism
Buddha	*c. 563–c. 483* B.C.E.	Buddhism
Jesus	*c. 8–4* B.C.E. *c. 29* C.E.	Christianity
Muhammad	*c. 570–c. 632* C.E.	Islam

a favorite horse that had become paralyzed, its legs drawn up into its body. Zarathushtra restored the horse to health, and made converts of Vishtaspa, his family, and his court. One who accepted Zarathushtra's preaching was Jamaspa, the kingdom's prime minister, who was to become Zarathushtra's spiritual successor. By this time Zarathushtra was forty-two years old.

The conversion of Vishtaspa proved to be a turning point. With the king's support and patronage, Zoroaster was free to preach and spread his message. Even then, things did not go smoothly. Rulers of the surrounding kingdoms attacked

---

■ Jamaspa's Promise

Jamaspa Hvogva, of wealth and power, and follower of Truth,

Doth choose for himself the wisdom of Thy Faith, O Lord,

And so choosing doth he attain to this great heritage,
  The Kingdom of the Good Mind.

Grant me, O Lord, that I may so teach people,

As ever to look for their shelter and protection in Thee,
  O Ahura.

—Ys. 51.18

Vishtaspa in an attempt to get him to renounce Zarathushtra's way. Fortunately for Zarathushtra and for Zoroastrianism, Vishtaspa and his sons were willing to fight for what they believed. Vishtaspa was forced to fight two wars in defense of Zoroastrianism. Vishtaspa's army proved to be a formidable fighting force. His general Isfendiyad defeated attackers and signed new treaties across Persia. Zarathushtra's message spread.

Zarathushtra's Later Life

Zarathushtra preached that people should live in the real world, working, marrying, and raising families. According to tradition, he himself married three times. By his first wife, whom he wed as a very young man, he had a son and three daughters; by his second wife, two sons. Only one wife, the last, is named in the Gathas—Hvovi.

The Gathas (13.98, 13.9) describe the wedding of Zarathushtra's youngest daughter, Pouruchista, to Jamaspa, the prime minister of Vishtaspa, as an occasion of much joy. In keeping with his belief that people should choose freely among the options in their lives, Zarathushtra speaks to his daughter about Jamaspa's good qualities, but allows her to choose for herself. Pouruchista responds:

> "Verily, I have chosen him,
> Faithful to my father and to my husband,
> Faithful to the peasants as to the nobles,
> Faithful as a righteous woman should be to the righteous,
> Mine shall be the glorious heritage—
> The light of the Good Mind;
> May Ahura Mazda grant me this blessing that endureth
>   for all time."

With the marriage of Pouruchista and Jamaspa, a new generation of Zarathushtis began.

The Death of Zarathushtra

Zarathushtra lived into old age. Zoroastrianism was spreading across the Persian landscape. But the new religion still had its detractors, particularly the priests of the old religion that Zoroastrianism was replacing. At age seventy-seven, Zarathushtra was preaching at Balkh when the place was attacked and he was killed. Some say that he was assassinated with a ritual dagger by a priest of the old order who could not bear to have Zarathushtra's message spread in the world; others say that he died at the hands of the soldiers. But the Zoroastrian fire could not be quenched. By the end of his life, Zarathushtra's message had taken root. It was to spread not only throughout Persia, but to have a far-reaching influence on other world religions as well.

CHAPTER 3

Zoroastrianism Through History

Zoroastrianism began and flourished on the Iranian Plain, in the land that became Persia, one of the great civilizations of the ancient world. But the history of Zoroastrianism goes back much further than the Persian Empire. By the time Persian culture reached its height, between the sixth and fourth centuries B.C.E., Zoroastrianism was already many centuries old.

Probably more than a thousand years passed between the time when Zarathushtra lived and the time when any history of the land and its peoples began to be written down. Even then, written history came not from the Persians, who left few written records of their own, but from the Greeks and other outside sources. Most of what we know today about the Persians and their time comes from Greek writings, from archaeological and language studies, and from the Avesta, the Zoroastrian holy book, which preserved oral history and legends.

Scholars believe that the people who settled the Iranian Plain migrated there between 2000 and 1500 B.C.E. from what is now southern Russia. From studying their languages, we know that they were of European, or Aryan, background, rather than

from the Middle East. The land the travelers found was unwelcoming—high, rugged mountains surrounded a dry salt desert. It was a land that was blisteringly hot in summer and frigid in winter. People gathered in the low valleys and along rivers, where they could farm and herd animals.

The migrants formed tribes. Mixing with the people who were already living in the areas they settled, and widely separated from other migrant groups, they developed distinct dialects. The two largest tribes were the Medes, in the land called Media to the north, and the Persians in the south, but there were others. Each was made up of smaller subgroups. Many, including the group into which Zarathushtra was born, apparently lived peacefully, farming and herding cattle and other livestock, the mainstay of their existence.

The migrants brought their rituals and beliefs with them from a still older time. The early Iranians practiced an ancient, polytheistic religion about which we know little. But its rituals included animal sacrifice and the use of intoxicating drugs to appease angry gods. Some of these rituals also served as a way to prepare young men for battle by rousing them into a state of frenzy. These young men formed warrior societies that crossed and recrossed the plains on horseback, raiding and plundering, stealing cattle and laying waste to farmland. So although many tribes lived peacefully, the times were scarred by violence and cruelty.

Early Zoroastrianism

The Prophet Zarathushtra came as a reformer to change the practices of the ancient Iranian religion. He preached against the excesses of ritual that led to drunken raiding and the senseless slaughter of cattle. His message was that people should focus their thoughts on one wise and good God, Ahura Mazda. Eventually, Zoroastrianism took root in the kingdom of Kai Vishtaspa, around Balkh, a city in Bactria, to the northeast.

Vishtaspa was one of the rulers of the legendary Kayanian dynasty that ruled in Iran in prehistory. We know little about him except that he adopted the new religion preached by Zarathushtra and that he was willing to defend his belief by fighting for it. Vishtaspa's support enabled Zoroastrianism to grow.

After Zarathushtra's death, the leadership of the new religion passed to Zarathushtra's son-in-law, Jamaspa, an official of Vishtaspa's court. Gradually, the religion moved outward from Vishtaspa's kingdom into other parts of Persia. For a thousand years after Zarathushtra's lifetime, Zoroastrianism continued to spread across the Iranian Plain.

Zoroastrianism Grows and Changes

The Zoroastrianism that developed in the centuries after Zarathushtra's death changed in some ways from the Prophet's original vision. For one thing, Zarathushtra had preached against the excesses of the ancient rituals. But as Zoroastrianism became more widely accepted, ritual returned. No longer, however, was its purpose to appease warlike gods and whip soldiers into a frenzy for battle. The rituals of Zoroastrianism focused on praising and worshiping Ahura Mazda. Many rituals of Zoroastrianism reached back to the ancient Iranian religion that had gone before it. This is not surprising, since Zarathushtra had been a reformer of the old religion, not the founder of a whole new religion. While boldly new in many ways, it had retained familiar elements, and returning to the old rituals seemed a natural step for its followers.

One ritual that returned involved the plant haoma. No one today is sure what plant had been used by the ancient priests. But in the new Haoma rite, it was ritually pounded to give up its juice. Mixed with milk, it was offered to Ahura Mazda, and small quantities were used by priests to help them obtain visions seeking the path of truth. The Haoma ritual became one of the main rites of Zoroastrianism.

As Zoroastrianism swept westward, it encountered the Magi, a priestly tribe of Medes. The Magi had long held the secrets of priestly ritual for the Median people. They were also the keepers of medical lore and of the knowledge of astronomy. Sometime around the eighth century, they adopted Zoroastrianism and claimed Zarathushtra as one of their own. They brought additional ritual practices to the religion, along with their knowledge of the stars. It was the Magi who first presented the teachings of Zarathushtra to the Greeks. Christians

SCS BALTHASSAR +SCS MELCHIOR +SCS GASPAR

■ *Tradition holds that the Three Wise Men who followed the star to Bethlehem to see the infant Jesus were Magi, or Zoroastrian priests. Zoroastrian children today enact the journey of the Magi at Christmastime.*

recognize the Zoroastrian priests as the Magi, the "Three Wise Men" who followed a star to Bethlehem to see the infant Jesus.

Zoroastrianism changed in other ways as well. Zarathushtra had not given bodily form to concepts of good and evil and to the Amesha Spentas. But in the following centuries, these abstract ideas became more concrete. The Amesha Spentas became the Beneficent Immortals, archangels that fought alongside Ahura Mazda in the battle against evil. Evil itself was given a name— Angra Mainyu, the Lie. Now people could visualize more easily the struggle between Truth and the Lie. Other ideas became concrete, too. People told of Ahura Mazda's creation of the world, and this, too, became part of Zoroastrian belief.

Cyrus the Great and the Achaemenid Empire

In 575 B.C.E., a Persian royal child was born. Young Cyrus showed an early talent for leadership. In 559, he ascended to the

Persian throne. A powerful Median kingdom had ruled the Persians for more than a century, but its influence was waning. The Median ruler challenged the young Persian king to battle in 549, and Cyrus defeated him. Cyrus took control of Media. Eventually his armies conquered the lands from Babylonia to the south, and up into central Asia to the north. His defeat of Babylon freed the Jews, in bondage there to the Babylonian king. Cyrus was widely revered by the Jewish people for his wisdom and generosity. Zoroastrianism is widely believed to have mingled with Judaism at this time, influencing the Jewish religion. This was the era of the great Hebrew prophet Isaiah, who preached of a savior yet to be born into the world, an idea that previously had been Zoroastrian alone.

It is not possible to say with certainty that Cyrus was a follower of the Zarathushtrian religion, although he may have been. Except for some official decrees, no written records of his reign survive, and Zoroastrianism is not mentioned by name in the Greek trading records of the time. But Zarathushtis point to his rule of justice and truth and the fact that he never tried to convert the peoples he conquered as signs that he was following the path laid down by Zarathushtra.

The Achaemenids

The imperial line Cyrus began is called the Achaemenid Empire, after his ancestor Achaemenes. After Cyrus's death, a century of fighting and warfare under a succession of Achaemenid rulers expanded Persian rule still further, from the Mediterranean Sea and into Africa on the west, and to the Indus River on the east.

■ Achaemenid Monarchs	
Cyrus the Great 559–529 B.C.E.	Artaxerxes I 465–425 B.C.E.
Cambyses 529–522 B.C.E.	Darius II 425–405 B.C.E.
Smerdis 522–521 B.C.E.	Artaxerxes II 425–359 B.C.E.
Darius I 521–485 B.C.E.	Artaxerxes III 359–340 B.C.E.
Xerxes 485–465 B.C.E.	Darius III 340–333 B.C.E.

The Achaemenids were not only fierce warriors. They were excellent managers, diplomatic in their approach to government, who administered their far-flung holdings with uncommon wisdom and foresight. Within the Persian domain was a well-developed communications system so that royal decrees could reach the farthest outposts in a matter of days. The Achaemenids traded widely within and outside their empire, particularly with the Greeks. Importantly, conquered tribes were allowed to keep their own religions and customs, a practice that helped to keep the peace. For example, the Magi, priests of the defeated Medes, gained favor with the Achaemenid court and became the chief priests of Zoroastrianism.

In 522 B.C.E., Darius I became emperor. Darius continued to emphasize military power and gained an international reputation for his rule of law. He also constructed roads and established a money system of gold coins. He built two palaces, the winter palace at Susa and the summer palace at Persepolis, famous for its architecture and lavish beauty.

Evidence suggests that Darius was indeed a Zoroastrian. His palace at Persepolis includes a relief of the winged Faravahar symbol. Another building in the ruins of Persepolis is believed to have been a fire temple. In addition, inscriptions from his reign give credit for his rule to the favor of Ahura Mazda. Xerxes, the son of Darius who followed his father on the throne, similarly spoke of worshiping Ahura Mazda and of banning the worship of *daevas*, the old Iranian gods, which were considered evil.

Originally all Zoroastrian worship had been held out of doors, around open fires. As foreign influences entered the Iranian Plain, however, probably in the fifth century B.C.E., people had begun to construct buildings so that they could hold their rituals in private.

Persia Under Alexander

After two hundred years on the throne, the Achaemenids were no longer as powerful as they had been. In Greece, the emperor Alexander saw a chance to extend his empire by overcoming Persia. He attacked with a huge army, and finally defeated the Persians under Darius III in 330 B.C.E. Alexander was ruthless in victory. He looted and burned the palace at Persepolis, stripping gold off the walls to finance his march across Persia. Although the rest of the world calls him "Alexander the Great," to Zoroastrians he became Alexander "the accursed," a name associated with Ahriman or Angra Mainyu, the evil spirit himself.

Alexander's invasion was a disaster for Zoroastrianism. The army destroyed fire temples and slaughtered priests. Centuries of Zoroastrian learning were lost. The Zoroastrians were no longer the ruling class with a powerful priesthood. The religion was left leaderless and in disarray.

After Alexander: The Seleucids

After Alexander's death in 323 B.C.E., his empire was divided. In 330 B.C.E., Persia was handed over to Seleucus I. The Seleucids put up temples to their own Greek gods and tried to encourage Greek culture in Persia, but their attempts were mostly unsuccessful. The Persians were fiercely proud, and their hatred of the Greeks ran deep. In name, the Greeks ruled Persia, but in practice, people regathered in tribes, and many small kingdoms emerged. The Greek religion never replaced Zoroastrianism, which seemed, if anything, to grow stronger.

Preoccupied with wars in Egypt and other parts of the Middle Eastern world, the Seleucids gradually lost control of the vast Iranian land. By 250 B.C.E., their influence was failing. The Parthians, an Iranian tribe to the north near the Caspian Sea, declared themselves a separate state. They raised an army and defended themselves successfully against Seleucid attempts to subdue them.

Parthian Rule

The Parthian ruler Mithridates I gradually gained control over all the Seleucid holdings in Persia during the second century B.C.E. His son Mithridates II extended his rule into India to the east and as far as Syria to the south and west.

The Parthians considered themselves the heirs of the Achaemenids. Like the Achaemenids, they practiced Zoroastrianism. They reconstructed fire temples that were destroyed by Alexander. In the oil-rich ground of the north, fire often occurred naturally, springing, as if miraculously, from the ground. The Parthian priests declared such places sacred and held fire rituals there. Greek influence waned. By now Zoroastrianism, already well over a thousand years old, was well established all across Persia among the ordinary people as well as in the ruling establishment.

Parthian Persia was tolerant of religions and home to many faiths. Hindus, Buddhists, Greeks, Jews, Christians, and pagans mixed there. Under the Parthians, Zoroastrianism itself had great variety. In a huge country with little communication, many ways of practicing the religion had developed. Some people worshiped Ahura Mazda in fire temples, others turned back to Mithra, an ancient god who became one of the archangels of Zoroastrian belief. Some temples had statues of the deity Anahita, a female deity. The Parthian kings themselves followed a form of the religion that had grown up in the east, but they did not try to impose their beliefs on the people. Instead, they were tolerant of all forms of worship.

In the first century C.E., the Parthian rulers began collecting the Avestan materials that had been scattered during Alexander's invasion and writing them down. Some materials, like the Gathas, had survived more or less intact. Others were in bits and pieces, fragments of different rituals and beliefs. The Parthians set about gathering everything they could find.

Centuries of warfare with the Romans weakened the Parthians, who were overrun by Roman armies for more than eighty years before they finally gave way in 198 C.E. The Parthian royal line continued, but with little power. On the whole, however, Parthian rule had helped to strengthen Zoroastrianism.

The Sasanians

As the Parthians declined, another Persian empire was on the rise. This one was ruled by Ardashir, the grandson of Sasan. Ardashir also claimed to be descended from the Achaemenids.

■ *The tomb of the Achaemenid emperor Cyrus the Great in the ruins at Pasargadae, Iran.*

He defeated the last of the Parthian kings in 224 C.E. and gradually consolidated his power over what had been their territory. Once he had brought all the Iranian kings and subkings under his control, Ardashir took on Rome. Shapur I, Ardashir's son, continued his work, defeating the Roman emperor Valerian in 259.

In matters of religion in general and Zoroastrianism in particular, the Sasanids thought the Parthians had been too liberal. To discourage the bubbling mix of religions on their soil, they made Zoroastrianism the official state religion. Then they set about standardizing it. Under the Parthians, followers of different priestly traditions had developed varying forms of ritual and belief. The Sasanids decided that there should be only one. They created a national priesthood to examine the materials the Parthians had collected and to do away with any ritual forms they felt were not "pure." Through this priestly editing, a standardized form of Zoroastrianism appeared. Some variety and vigor were necessarily lost, and the religion became more concerned with ritual than it had previously been, but now it was clear what was and was not Zoroastrian.

Gathering the Avesta

The Sasanids continued the work of collecting and writing down the Avestan literature. They developed a special script in which to record the Gathic Avestan dialect spoken by Zarathushtra as well as Zoroastrian texts in the later, but still very ancient "Young Avestan," both of which had been preserved exactly in Zoroastrianism's long oral tradition.

Until the time of the Sasanians, the written language of Zoroastrianism had been Avestan. The spoken language, however, had been changing and developing. The language the Persian people spoke was what is called *Pahlavi*, or Middle Persian. The name of Ahura Mazda, for example, became Ohrmazd, and Angra Mainyu, the evil spirit, became Ahriman. Sasanid scribes not only copied down the ancient Gathic texts, but they translated them into the language spoken by the masses so that Pahlavi speakers could understand them without special knowledge.

The Sasanids also recorded other traditions of Zoroastrianism, such as the creation of the world and humankind, and they added commentaries, or *Zand,* to the growing body of literature that was the Avesta.

Zoroastrianism in the Later Sasanian Period

As the official state religion, Zoroastrianism occupied a special place in Sasanian Persia. However, by now Zoroastrianism had to compete with other religions that had made their way into Persia. Although these faiths were officially banned, the rigid, state-sponsored form of Zoroastrianism caused some people to turn to other beliefs. A new prophet, a young man named Mani, caught the ear of one of the Sasanid rulers. Mani's religion, called Manichaeism, was a blend of Zoroastrian, Christian, Buddhist, and Gnostic beliefs (Gnosticism was an offshoot of early Christianity). When the next ruler came into power, though, Mani fell into disfavor. He was imprisoned and later put to death. Without its leader, Manichaeism's influence faded. Another sect, with communistic overtones, arose under a leader named Mazdak, but this too was put down. Although Christianity continued to spread in the west, Zoroastrianism in its Sasanian form remained the religion of the Persian people and their kings.

■ *Historical Periods*

Achaemenid Empire 550 B.C.E.–330 B.C.E.

Selucid Empire 330 B.C.E.–250 B.C.E.

Parthian Dynasty 250 B.C.E.–226 C.E.

Sasanian Dynasty 226 C.E.–641 C.E.

Muslim Conquest

In 637 C.E., the Arabs attacked Persia and overwhelmed the Sasanian army. Sasanian kings remained on the throne until 652. The last of the Sasanian rulers, a young king named Yazdegard III, had taken over an empire in turmoil. Ten rulers had preceded him in the previous five years, as the Arab threat grew.

Yazdegard tried to fight, but as Arab victories multiplied, his situation became increasingly hopeless. He turned for help to the governor of Merv, but the governor betrayed him to the Arab forces. He was tracked down and murdered at the age of thirty-four. The four-hundred year reign of the Sasanids came to an end. Muslim rulers took over Persia.

Zoroastrianism Under Muslim Rule

Islam swept the country along with the Muslim rulers. Many people converted voluntarily, recognizing in Islam familiar concepts of Zoroastrianism such as heaven and hell, a final judgment, and prayer at regular intervals five times a day. But stories remain of Zoroastrians being forced to convert at sword-point. Until the ninth century, however, Zoroastrianism was still the majority religion. Scholarly Zoroastrian priests continued to write commentaries on the Avesta in Pahlavi, adding to Zoroastrian knowledge. But Islam was firmly established. Ruling powers used a combination of persuasion, economic pressure, and force to convert everybody to Islam. By the late ninth century, the Zoroastrian faithful were finding life increasingly hard.

■ *Islam Comes to Bukhara*

After the Muslim invasion, the city of Bukhara remained steadfastly Zoroastrian, worshiping in their fire temples on their holy days. Three different times, the Muslim ruler, Qutaiba ibn Muslim, made war on the city and converted the people, and all three times after he left, they returned to Zoroastrianism. The fourth time, Qutaiba made sure that there would be no backsliding. He made Zoroastrianism difficult for the people in every way possible. He ordered them to give half of their homes to Arabs, who could watch and inform on them. He built mosques and destroyed fire temples. He severely punished people who broke Muslim religious laws and rewarded those who came to Friday prayer with gifts of money. Outside the city, wealthy Zoroastrians in their villas still resisted. When soldiers called them to Friday prayer, they threw stones at them from their rooftops. Finally they were overcome by military force...

—Adapted from *Textual Sources for the Study of Zoroastrianism* by Mary Boyce, 1984.

Around the tenth century, a group of devout Zarathushtis and their priests fled Persia to settle in India, where they became known as Parsis. Those who stayed behind all but disappeared as an influence on Iranian culture.

In the thirteenth century, Zoroastrians who remained faithful fled their homes to the cities of Yazd and Kirman, where they practiced their religion in secret. For a time, the Muslims left them alone, and they were able to live as craftspeople and farmers. But in the sixteenth century another wave of forced conversion took place. Zoroastrians moved to Isfahan, where they worked as laborers. In the early seventeenth century, there was an Afghani invasion, followed not long after by an invasion when the Qajar dynasty seized power. In these two periods of warfare, more than one hundred thousand Zoroastrians were killed.

Zoroastrian Fortunes in the Nineteenth Century

By the nineteenth century, the plight of the Zoroastrians, or Zartoshtis, in Iran was dire indeed. Only about twelve thousand were left. Although classified as an official minority, they were persecuted. Muslim rulers levied a heavy tax called *jizya* on all non-Muslims. This tax effectively impoverished the Zoroastrian community. Iranian law heaped indignities on the vanishing population. Zartoshtis were not allowed to travel and were forced to wear clothing made of undyed cloth. Laws banned them from touching food in the markets. They were forbidden to ride horses, and if they had the misfortune to be riding a donkey when a Muslim came by, they had to get down and walk. Zartoshti men were barred from wearing turbans, which made them instantly recognizable as *gabars* or "infidels"—nonbelievers—and subject to harassment and humiliation. Zoroastrians had no legal standing: a Muslim who killed a Zoroastrian faced no penalty. Yet in spite of overwhelming hardship, Zoroastrians persisted in their religion. Despite Iranian society's efforts to wipe it out, Iranian Zoroastrianism continued.

Meanwhile in India, the Parsi community was flourishing. In 1882, the Parsis sent an influential Parsi named Manekji Hataria to Iran to lobby the Qajar rulers on behalf of the Iranian Zoroastrians. Hataria's mission was at least partly successful.

The repressive jizya was lifted, and poverty eased. Soon after, education and better medical care became available. By the early 1900s, Zartoshtis had begun to open businesses and improve their position in Iranian life. It took less than half a century for them to reverse hundreds of years of repression and become active in banking, education, engineering, and the professions.

Modern Iran

Meanwhile, in Iran at large, corruption and weak government led to continual unrest. A series of uprisings caused the old Qajar dynasty to collapse. World War I only added to the confusion as power swung back and forth.

In 1925, a new dynasty, headed by Reza Shah Pahlavi, took control. Reza Shah was a strong leader who consolidated political power and brought about reforms. His policies were

■ *The Shah of Iran on the Peacock throne. Although Muslim, the shahs were sympathetic to the Iranian Zoroastrians, calling them "the true Persians" and using the example of Zoroastrian steadfastness to instill national pride.*

largely continued by his son, Mohammed Reza Pahlavi, who followed him on the Peacock Throne in 1941.

Under the Pahlavi reign, the fortunes of the Zoroastrians continued to improve. The shahs moved to control Muslim religious influences and pointed to the small but durable band of Zartoshtis still surviving in Iran as the "true Persians." With the new pride in Zoroastrianism, people whose families had been Muslim for centuries returned to the Zoroastrianism of their ancestors.

Pahlavi rule, however, had its own problems. As troubles multiplied, the shah's policies became harsher and the people more restless. In 1979, many opponents of the shah united under the Ayatollah Ruhollah Khomeinei, a Muslim religious leader. He and his followers declared Iran to be an Islamic Republic and established a new government based on the teachings of Islam.

With the return of a Muslim-ruled government, many restrictions were placed on people's personal freedoms. This was especially the case for many Zoroastrians who had enjoyed improved status under the shah. The crackdown caused many of them to leave Iran. Citing the threat of religious persecution, they migrated to Britain, Australia, Canada, and the United States, among other countries. The Islamic Republic officially maintains Zoroastrianism as a "protected minority" in Iran, and the persecution that the Zoroastrian community feared has not happened. Zoroastrians may not work for the government, for example, but they are respected in other areas of Iranian life. An unknown number of Iranian Muslims each year "revert" to Zoroastrianism. Although this is officially illegal, there seem to have been no problems. Nevertheless, in a country overwhelmingly Muslim, educational and professional opportunities for Zoroastrians are somewhat limited, and the threat of persecution remains.

CHAPTER **4**

Zoroastrianism in India: The Parsis

After the Arab invasion in 642 C.E., life was increasingly harsh for Zoroastrians. In 651, the Arabs overthrew the last Persian emperor, Yazdegard III, and took over the Persian throne. Over the next two hundred years, the Muslim rulers made conversion to Islam a priority. For those who would not give up their Zarathushti religion, the penalties multiplied.

A group of Zarathushti priests and believers abandoned their homes and their temple. Carrying the consecrated fire with them, they withdrew to the Khorasan Mountains, where they formed a community. For a time they lived peacefully, but eventually they were discovered and persecuted there as well. They left the mountains and settled in the town of Hormuz, near the Persian Gulf. But once again, they were harassed. Finally, one of their priests advised them that if they were to survive as a Zoroastrian community, they would have to leave Persia.

The Zarathushtis sailed from Hormuz to Diu, an island off the coast of northern India. They stayed in Diu for a time, usually given as nineteen years. Then, on the advice of one of their priests, they set sail again, this time for the Indian state of Gujarat.

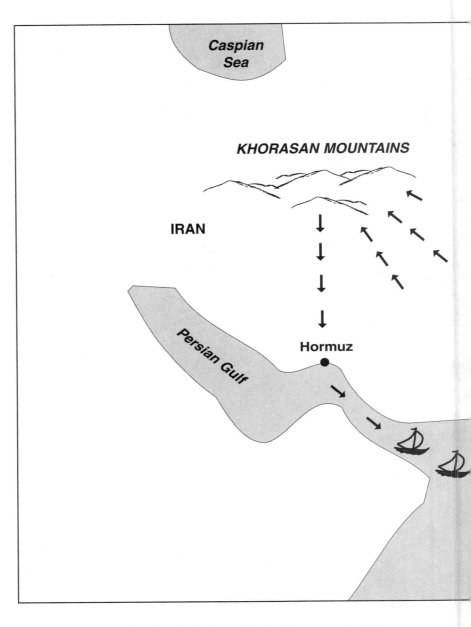

Far out in the Gulf, the Zarathushtis met a terrible storm that threatened to swamp the boats and take them all to the bottom. Battered by winds and waves and in desperate fear for their lives, the travelers prayed to Ahura Mazda for a safe harbor and promised to build a holy fire temple if they reached land alive.

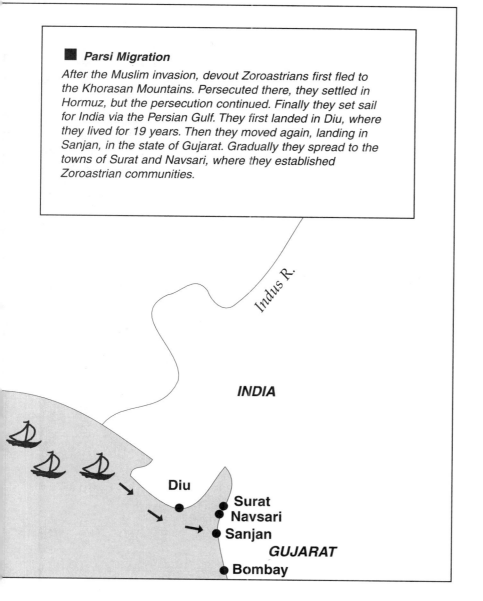

Parsi Migration

After the Muslim invasion, devout Zoroastrians first fled to the Khorasan Mountains. Persecuted there, they settled in Hormuz, but the persecution continued. Finally they set sail for India via the Persian Gulf. They first landed in Diu, where they lived for 19 years. Then they moved again, landing in Sanjan, in the state of Gujarat. Gradually they spread to the towns of Surat and Navsari, where they established Zoroastrian communities.

Indus R.

INDIA

Diu

Surat
Navsari
Sanjan

GUJARAT

Bombay

The winds subsided, and they landed in Sanjan, a port north of what is now the city of Bombay. The actual date of their migration is uncertain. It is usually given as 936 C.E. but sometimes earlier. Probably there were a number of migrations through the ninth and tenth centuries.

■ *An Atash Bahram in the Indian seaside village of Udwada. This is considered the most holy of all the Atash Bahrams in India.*

According to tradition, the chief priest, or *Dastur*, approached the local Hindu ruler, Jadi Rana, for asylum. He asked for only three things: the freedom to practice their religion, the freedom to bring up their children according to their own custom, and a small piece of land.

The Parsis tell that Jadi Rana offered the Zoroastrians a pitcher of milk that was full to the brim, by way of explaining that his realm was already crowded. The Zoroastrian leader added a pinch of sugar to the milk, to suggest that the Zarathushtis would fit in and enrich the country. Jadi Rana granted the Zarathushtis' requests on five conditions:

- They must educate the ruler about the Zarathushti religion.
- They must give up their Persian language and speak only Gujarati, the local language.
- The women must adopt Indian dress and wear the sari.
- The men must give up their weapons.
- They must agree to hold their weddings only in the evening so as not to conflict with Hindu ceremonies.

The Dastur agreed to the terms. In return, the Zarathushtis, whom the local people called "Parsis" because they had come from the Iranian province of Pars, received the land they had asked for. They immediately set about building their temple, an Atash Behram, in which to place their sacred fire. The fire, since it could not be safely carried in the boats, had to be brought overland across the mountains, as did the consecrated tools for building the temple.

Life in India

Over the next centuries, the Zoroastrian community flourished. They stayed to themselves and did not seek converts, but the community grew steadily. One reason was that they had very large families. They made their living as farmers and merchants. Gradually they spread out from Sanjan into the surrounding areas. Wherever they went, they built fire temples and worshiped Ahura Mazda. In towns along the coast, Parsis took up shipbuilding and other trades. Hardworking and scrupulously honest, they won the respect of the people with whom they worked.

Around 1297, Muslim invaders advanced on the Sanjan area. Fourteen hundred Zarathushti men joined the Hindu army to fight off the attack. After days of bloody fighting in which the battle seesawed back and forth, Sanjan fell to the Muslims. The Zoroastrians fled to the nearby mountain of Bahrot. For the next twelve years, they preserved their sacred fire in the caves of Bahrot, and then moved it to a hill near what is now the town of Bulsar. Over the next hundred years, the Zarathushtis drifted back into the area along the Gulf of Cambay, where they had long been established. In 1419, priests moved the holy fire to Navsari. It remained there for three hundred years.

From 1737 to 1742, the sacred fire was moved from one town to another, as priests disagreed over where it should be lodged. In 1742, the Zarathushtis of Udvada built an Atash Behram there, and moved the sacred fire to a permanent home. By this time, the Zarathushtis had been in India for over seven hundred years.

Meanwhile, Parsis established themselves in business and trade. They were trading with the Portuguese in the fifteenth century, and by the mid-1700s Parsi merchants had traveled to China to establish trade links there. In spite of their cosmopolitan contacts, however, they clung to their Zoroastrian religious tradition. Parsis did, however, adopt certain Hindu social customs. By the late seventeenth century, Parsi society was organized along the lines of a Hindu caste, led by a *panchayat,* a group of community leaders. The panchayat settled disputes and made rulings about social issues, such as family quarrels, property arguments, and divorce settlements. They also managed community property and trusts. Priests handled religious matters, however.

Keeping the Faith: The Rivyats

The Parsi community spoke Gujarati, the language of the part of India in which they lived, but they still used Pahlavi as a ritual language. Priests learned the ancient texts by heart, although by now few people fully understood their meaning.

Even though they had given up their language and many of their Persian customs for Indian ones, the Parsis still looked to the Zarathushti priests as the authorities on their religion. Through the sixteenth century, they corresponded with the priests of Kirman and Yazd, the last centers of Zoroastrianism left in Iran. The high priest, or *Dasturan Dastur,* of Yazd, in particular, who had gathered a religious community of priests around him, was considered to be the best source of religious knowledge. The Parsis wrote to the Dastur with their questions on matters of orthodox belief and ritual and received answers. The *Parsi Rivyats,* or "letters," span nearly a century and became part of Zoroastrian literature.

Parsis Under British Rule

Since the early 1700s, the British had been exercising commercial and political power in India. By 1815, India had become part of the British Empire. The British Raj—a Hindu word meaning "reign"—controlled India for the next sixty years.

When the British took control of India, Parsis were already well established in the city of Bombay. They had begun moving to the city to trade with the Portuguese in the fifteenth century. By 1672, they had a temple and a *dakhma,* a structure for disposing of their dead, there. In the late 1700s, drought in Gujarat made farming unprofitable, and many more Parsis migrated to Bombay. Always industrious, they found jobs in business and banking. The Parsis were not bound by the Hindu caste system, which made upward mobility difficult for Hindus. They established themselves quickly and began to rise in importance in Indian cultural and economic life.

Parsis were popular with employers because of their truthfulness and reliability. Their religion taught them to live fully in society and to fight worldly evils such as illness and poverty. What better way than to succeed economically, to have the money and power to do good in the world?

Besides, Parsis had always stayed to themselves. They had maintained their Persian identity and never felt strongly Indian. Strangers in India themselves, even after hundreds of years, they

■ *A Parsi mother and children in traditional Parsi Gujarati dress.*

had no reason to resent British rule. On the contrary, they welcomed the opportunities the British offered in education and business. They were quick to study and learn English, which made them even more desirable to the British. From the British standpoint, the Parsis were welcome as both workers and friends. The Hindus, who neither drank wine nor ate meat, refused British hospitality. The Parsis were pleasant and sociable. Parsis soon gained economic strength that was considerably greater than their numbers in the Indian population would suggest was possible. Many owned their own prosperous businesses. Some credit the Parsis with having a special genius for business, but more likely their success was driven by the strong work ethic of Zoroastrianism and their respect for learning.

Parsi women also benefited from British rule. The British offered educational opportunities for women that had not been widely available before, and Parsis enrolled their daughters in record numbers. Although Iranian, and later Indian, society had placed restrictions on women, Zoroastrianism placed women on a par with men in matters of religion and education. Parsi families welcomed the chance to educate their daughters.

In general the Parsis thrived, but they did encounter difficulties. In 1851, Indian Muslims took exception to something that appeared in a Parsi publication, and riots broke out. Parsi homes and businesses were damaged and looted. A similar event occurred in 1874, when Muslims attacked Parsi fire temples. At the end of the century, an epidemic of bubonic plague killed thousands of people, Muslim, Hindu, and Parsi alike.

On the whole, however, the Parsis prospered. They were hardworking and quick to adopt new ideas. A number of Parsis amassed fortunes in such areas as shipbuilding, international trading, textiles, iron and steel, and engineering. It was a Parsi, Jehangir Ratan D. Tata, who won the first pilot's license ever issued in India and founded India's first air service, Tata Aviation, which later became Air India. Parsis established the first wireless service, which linked India to Britain by radio for the first time. A Parsi scientist was responsible for India's atomic energy program. Parsis founded the Bombay Symphony. Parsis also excelled in areas such as law and education.

At the same time, Parsis were quick to reach out to those less fortunate than themselves. Along with their reputation as shrewd but honest businesspeople, they became known for their generous giving to charitable causes. Zoroastrianism teaches that anyone who fights the evils of society, such as illness, poverty, and ignorance, is working with Ahura Mazda toward perfecting the world. Parsis became known for philanthropy. The most successful Parsi businesspeople were also the most generous. Parsi money built much of modern Bombay. Besides erecting more than 160 fire temples, they donated primary funding to house the poor and to build many hospitals, schools, libraries, and institutes of science and art. When disaster struck anywhere in the country, Parsis were among the first to send aid. They provided scholarships and built cultural halls and museums, not just for Parsis, but open to all.

Parsis in Modern Times

For more than fifty years before India gained independence, the Indian National Movement had been trying to win freedom from British rule. A number of Parsis were active in the movement, both as elected officials who spoke for Indian nationalism and as spokespeople for Indian freedom. Perhaps

■ *Conductor Zubin Mehta, in performance.*

even more important than political efforts, Parsi business and industry served to help India become economically strong, making independence possible. India won its independence at

the close of World War II. At that time, India was partitioned into India, which today is strongly Hindu, and Pakistan, which is mainly Muslim.

With the withdrawal of the British from India, the Parsis lost some of their favored status. The Hindu National Party became the ruling political power. Parsis were once again only a small minority in a huge country. Moreover, the partition of India divided the already small Parsi population in India by making the Parsis in the north Pakistani citizens. However, Parsis still had considerable economic strength and energy. Today they participate in every aspect of Indian business and culture. Parsis have immigrated to North America, Europe, or

Australia in search of educational opportunities and jobs in technical fields. Wherever they go, they work to maintain their commitment to their religion.

Parsis are, and have always been, exclusive. To conservative Parsis, their faith is a God-given birthright that cannot be acquired from the outside. Parsis consider themselves a distinct ethnic group. According to a 1906 ruling by the Bombay High Court, people who are not born of two Parsi parents or who come to Zoroastrianism from outside the religion may become Zoroastrians, but they can never consider themselves Parsis. Parsis are only those people who are descended from the original Persian immigrants. The only exception is that the children of Parsi fathers by non-Parsi mothers may be accepted into the faith. The children of Parsi mothers by non-Parsi fathers may not. Only "true" Parsis—that is, active believers who were born of two Parsi parents—may enter the presence of a consecrated fire or observe the highest Zoroastrian rites. Many Parsis feel deeply that marrying only within the faith is one of the main things that has kept their religion alive for more than three thousand years, and permitting intermarriage weakens the religion.

The basic debate is one that asks: "Who is a Parsi?" For some, a Parsi is one who belongs primarily to an ethnic group, that is, Zoroastrians of the Iranian diaspora. For others, a Parsi is anyone who follows a way of life dedicated to good thoughts, words, and deeds in accord with the spirit of the Master.

In today's world, modern demands have challenged traditional ways of defining people and their ethnic and religious identities. The Parsis of India have experienced this challenge even more than many other religious communities. They have the largest concentration of Zoroastrian believers in one place. Yet in today's world, they are still only .01 percent of the Indian population and need to find new means of preservation. They must work to maintain a traditional faith and to preserve the number of dedicated faithful followers. In a greatly changing world, they must also ask themselves what measures must they take to guarantee their survival and growth in such new and demanding circumstances.

CHAPTER 5

The Avesta: The Zoroastrian Scripture

*T*he Zoroastrian scripture is the Avesta. Its contents were created over many centuries reaching back into prehistory. The oldest part of the Avesta was composed in Gathic Avestan, the language of the Prophet Zarathushtra. The part of the Avesta in Gathic includes the seventeen hymns or psalms composed by Zarathushtra himself. Other sections of the Avesta are written in a slightly later, but still very ancient, form of Avestan that scholars call "Young Avestan" to distinguish it from Gathic Avestan.

Traditional Zarathushtis consider their sacred scriptures to have immense spiritual power. Not only do they teach truth, but merely to speak the Avestan words aloud or to hear them spoken by a priest is a special blessing that helps to fight evil and furthers the cause of Truth in the world. From the scriptures come the liturgy and daily prayers of Zarathushtis.

History of the Avesta

The Avesta began as an oral document, memorized and recited by priests. In Zarathushtra's place and time, writing was unknown, and priestly training generally required such feats of

■ **Names of Deities in the Languages of the Avesta**

Avestan	Pahlavi
Ahura Mazda	Ohrmazd, Hormazd
Spenta Mainyu	Spenag Menog
Angra Mainyu	Ahriman
Asha	Ardvahist
Vohu Mana	Vahman
Spenta Armaity	Aspandarmad
Khshathra Vairya	Shehrevar
Haurvatat	Khordad
Ameratat	Amardad
Mithra	Meher, Mehr

memory. Religious belief and ritual were never written down. Even when writing first appeared, it was used for recordkeeping and trade, not for composing literature, which was an oral art.

No one knows when scribes began to collect Zarathushtra's songs and commit them to writing. Tradition holds that in 330 B.C.E., when the Greek general Alexander burned the palace at Persepolis and its library, one of the treasures he destroyed was a complete copy of the Avesta, written in gold on twelve thousand goatskins. So total was the destruction that we will never know whether such a document actually existed. In any event, the effect of the Greek army's devastation on Zoroastrian learning was the same. Whatever Avestan writings were there were scattered and burned. In addition, a great many Zoroastrian priests were slaughtered by Alexander's army. The Avestan passages the priests had committed to memory died with them, never to be completely recalled.

Almost four hundred years later, in the first century C.E., when the Parthians were in power, a ruler set his scribes to collecting the scattered pieces of the Avesta. The work continued under the Sasanians. Through the fourth and fifth centuries C.E., they collected volumes of material that they assembled in a "Great Avesta." The work they produced included, not only all the Avestan texts, but translations and explanations of them in Pahlavi, their language. Copies were placed in the libraries of the leading fire temples.

The Sasanians were also responsible for collecting as much as they could of the "Lost Avesta." These were the parts of the Avesta that had presumably been destroyed by the Greeks, but which had survived in the oral tradition. The Lost Avesta passages provide important clues to the contents of the original Avesta. These, along with other Zoroastrian writings, they assembled in what is called the Zand.

In the seventh century, an invasion by the Arabs swept Persia, dethroning the Sasanians. Zoroastrianism suffered great losses. Scholar-priests continued the work of creating the Pahlavi Zand for at least two more centuries. In the end, though, invasions by the Turks and the Mongols completed the destruction begun by the Arabs. Temples were burned and their libraries with them. Not a single complete copy of the Great Avesta survived. However, enough of the ancient Avestan writings remained that they could once again be collected into the Avesta we know today. It is probably about one-fourth of the original.

Following the Arab conquest, the language, script, and religion of Persia changed completely. Zoroastrianism all but disappeared from the world's consciousness for the next thousand years. In 1755, a French scholar named Abraham Anquetil-Duperon came across Zoroastrianism in India. He published a translation of the Avesta in France in 1771. His efforts brought a knowledge of the Avesta to the modern world.

Contents of the Avesta

The sacred scripture of the Avesta is in six parts:
- *Yasna*, "sacrifice, worship." The main liturgical text. It includes the Gathas, the fundamental teachings of Zarathushtra.
- *Visperad*, "All the Lords." A liturgical text invoking Zoroastrian saints and heavenly beings, used on Zoroastrian holy days.
- *Yashts*, hymns of praise to Zoroastrian saints and angels, or *yazatas*. The Yashts praise many of the

deities from Iranian religion before Zarathushtra's reforms.

- *Vendidad,* a priestly code dealing mainly with rituals, regulations, and purification.
- Minor texts: *Khorda Avesta, Nyayesh, Gah,* etc. Short pieces, sometimes from other parts of the Avesta, used as prayers and invocations by both priests and laypeople.
- Fragments of the Lost Avesta. Prayers, invocations, and blessings.

The Yasna

The Avesta opens with the Yasna, or "sacrifice." It contains the Zoroastrian liturgy, the formal words spoken by priests during worship, including the creed of belief of all Zarathushtis and formal invocations for priests to speak as they perform various rituals. Parts of the Yasna form the daily prayers of all Zoroastrians. Some of the Yasna liturgy, such as the *Yasna Haptanhaiti,* is composed in Gathic Avestan, dating to Zarathushtra's time. Much, however, is in Young Avestan, as Zoroastrian liturgy probably developed over the centuries following Zarathushtra's lifetime, when Gathic was no longer spoken.

For Zarathushtis, a central part of the Yasna is the seventeen Gathic hymns that are the actual words of Zarathushtra. These seventeen Gathas, or psalms, occupy a very special place in Zoroastrianism. All Zoroastrian doctrine and belief are based on them.

The Gathas

Zarathushtra composed the Gathas throughout his lifetime, and he probably composed many more of them. The Gathas that have come down to us are probably only fragments of Zarathushtra's message. But they are enough to glimpse the power of his preaching and his poetic style, and to understand the vision he had of Ahura Mazda and the Good Religion. The Gathas probably survived in their original form because they were poems. Their rhythm and meter made them easier to memorize than prose, and also harder to change. Zarathushtra's own words provide one of the best ways to understand the fundamental beliefs of Zoroastrianism.

No one knows exactly in what order these hymns were composed, although there are some clues within them. Later scholars organized the seventeen Gathas believed to be by Zarathushtra into five groups within the Yasna, according to their meter:

- Ahunavaiti Gatha (Ys. 28–34)
- Ustavaiti Gatha (Ys. 43–46)
- Spenta Mainyu Gatha (Ys. 47–50)
- Vohu Khshathra Gatha (Ys. 51)
- Vahisto Ishti Gatha (Ys. 53)

In these passages, Zarathushtra lays down the basic principles of Zoroastrian faith, although not in a systematic or doctrinaire way. The Gathas are expressions of Zarathushtra's belief in and personal experience with God. Some are songs of praise to Ahura Mazda; others are prayers and thanksgiving; and some are dialogues with Ahura Mazda concerning universal questions of the meaning of life and how it is to be lived.

Ahunavaiti: Ys. 28–34

The Ahunavaiti Gathas open with a hymn to Ahura Mazda in which Zarathushtra prays for the gifts of righteousness and wisdom, that he may spread joy in the world:

> *In humble adoration, with hands outstretched,*
>   *I pray to thee, O Mazda*
> *Through Thy benevolent Spirit,*
> *Vouchsafe to me in this hour of joy*
> *All righteousness of action,*
>   *all wisdom of the Good Mind,*
> *That I may thereby bring joy to*
>   *the Soul of Creation. (Ys. 28.1)*

The next hymn, Ys. 29, is known as "The Lament of the Cow." Cattle were supremely important in Zarathushtra's culture. There was no part of them that could not be used—milk, meat, hide, bones, manure. People were enormously dependent on their cattle and felt a great kinship with them. An attack on a family's cattle was not much different from attacking the family itself.

Zarathushtra composes his hymn in the sorrowful voice of the Cow, which is laboring under warfare and unrest. For Zarathushtra and his listeners, the Cow represents the pastoral life being destroyed by warfare and violence. Its voice is the Soul of Creation. The lament is more touching coming from this poor voiceless creature that must suffer because of human greed and cruelty. The Soul of the Cow cries to Ahura Mazda for a protector. Ahura Mazda then turns to Zarathushtra, "The one who alone has hearkened to my command." The Soul has doubts. It asked for someone powerful, and Zarathushtra is neither a great king nor a great warrior, but a humble man. Even Zarathushtra is uncertain. Ahura Mazda prevails, however, and Zarathushtra sets out on his mission.

In Ys. 30.3, Zarathushtra begins to lay out his message to followers. He offers them the hope of heaven through following the path of Truth (Asha). He tells his listeners that there has always been evil in the world, but that people have within them the wisdom to choose good over evil:

> In the beginning there were two Primal Spirits,
>   Twins simultaneously active,
> These are the Good and the Evil, in thought,
>   and in word, and in deed.
> Between these two, let the wise one choose aright,
>   Be good, not base.

Evil destroys. It brings those who choose it nothing but misery. Those who choose good, however, are helping to move the world toward perfection and themselves toward eternal joy.

In Ys. 34, Zarathushtra addresses Ahura Mazda, asking the Lord to confirm his mission.

This Gatha was probably written when Zarathushtra was in middle age, after the religion had been adopted by Kai Vishtaspa and his court. The new faith was slow in catching on. Zarathushtra tells Ahura Mazda that his followers are following Asha, the path of Truth. Yet people still practice the old religion. Zarathushtra asks for reassurance:

What are thy commandments, and what doest thou
   desire, O Mazda?
What of invocation, what of worship?
Speak forth, my Lord, that I may hear thee!
That I may know what will bestow on us
   Thy Blessed rewards.
Teach me through the Good-Mind and the noble Path of
   Truth and Right. (Ys. 34.12.)

Yet even in his questioning, Zarathushtra is certain that all will be revealed through the Good Mind, so that humankind and Ahura Mazda can work together to further Ahura Mazda's plan.

Ustavaiti: Ys. 43–46

In the Ustavaiti Gathas, Zarathushtra asks Ahura Mazda questions having to do with the meaning of existence—questions that are central to all religious thought. In the version of the Avesta that has come down to us today, Zarathushtra answers some questions, but many are left open for followers to ponder.

This I ask Thee, tell me truly, O Ahura;
In the beginning, who was the father and creator of
   Asha, the Truth?
Who determined the paths of the sun and stars?
Who, but Thee, so arranged the moon to wax and wane?
This, O Mazda, and much more, I fain would know.
   (Ys. 44.3.)

The answer to the question seems obvious: Ahura Mazda. But by posing the thought as a question, Zarathushtra invites his listeners to answer for themselves. He also links Truth with such natural phenomena as the sun, moon, and stars, implying that it is a fundamental principle of all existence.

Zarathushtra goes on to ask many other questions of the human heart. How is it best to make the soul take the Good to itself? How is it best to praise Ahura Mazda? How can the religion be made to prosper? How may a righteous person be told from an unrighteous one? In questions such as these, he deals with the thorny issues that have plagued humankind through all

A page from the Avesta, written in Avestan script, with notes between the lines in Pahlavi, or Middle Persian. This page tells the story of the "Primal Twins," Truth and the Lie, before the beginning of time.

religious history. Finally, he asks how he may achieve the perfection of the Good Mind that he so earnestly seeks.

In Ys. 45, Zarathushtra delivers a sermon to his followers. He reminds them of the conflict between good and evil, which can "never agree." He has come to bring the message of Ahura Mazda, with the warning that for those who do not follow it, there will be eternal misery. What is best in life is to follow the spirit of Truth, Asha, and to live according to the Good Mind and good actions. Those who do this shall be blessed with perfection and immortality. In the final verse, Zarathushtra promises a personal relationship with Ahura Mazda:

> *Whoso shuns the evil-liars and those who shun*
> *the Lord*
> *Whoso reveres Him, the most High, through the*
> *holy faith of his appointed Savior,*
> *To him, O Mazda, Thou shalt be a friend, even*
> *brother and father!* (Ys. 45.11)

In the next Gatha of this group (Ys. 46), Zarathushtra reflects on his earlier life and difficulties. He recalls being deserted and rejected. At the time, he wondered aloud why his followers were so few and his message so little heard. Yet as the Gatha continues, it is clear that Zarathushtra was never close to giving up. He knows that the way of Asha is the Good Life and that those who refuse to follow it will come to grief in the end. He calls upon the people who rejected him to come to the Right. To those who follow Ahura Mazda, he proclaims:

> *He, who following Truth, shall work for me,*
> *Zarathushtra,*
> *To bring us toward the Great Renovation in accordance*
> *with Thy purpose,*
> *For him shall be all honor and content in this world,*
> *And a fitting state in the life beyond.*
> *As verily, Thou has revealed to me, O All-knowing*
> *Mazda.* (Ys. 46.19)

Spenta Mainyu: Ys. 47–50

The next group of psalms is short. It takes its name from the Spirit of Truth. Zarathushtra speaks to Ahura Mazda and to his followers. The tone of the poem suggests that these were not easy times. There are hints of political unrest. Zarathushtra expresses the hope that the righteous may win out over the unrighteous, and that the people be ruled by those who know how to rule well, not evil rulers. "When shall happy life in peaceful pastures come to us through good rule?" he asks (Ys. 48.11).

Yet at the end, he foresees a time when leaders appointed by Ahura Mazda will come to take away violence and bring Truth and Justice.

Vohu Khshathra: Ys. 51

In this Gatha, which relates to Ahura Mazda's power and might, Zarathushtra returns to the theme of what awaits the wicked, a trial by fire and molten metal that will destroy them. The souls of the wicked will be turned back at the Chinvat Bridge, the Bridge of the Separator, because they have wandered from the path of Truth. He mentions those who have become enlightened—his cousin Maidhyoimanha, the king Vishtaspa, and the members of the king's court, Frashaoshtra and Jamaspa—and asks that Ahura Mazda give them, and him, salvation.

Vahisto Ishti: Ys. 53

This Gatha tells of the wedding of Pouruchista, Zarathushtra's youngest daughter, to Jamaspa, an official in the court of Vishtaspa. Some scholars believe that this Gatha was composed by a follower of Zarathushtra rather than by Zarathushtra himself. However, it does provide a glimpse into life in Zarathushtra's time.

Although they are only a part of the body of psalms composed by Zarathushtra, the Gathas form a unified picture of his message. People can find salvation by serving Ahura Mazda through the goodness of their lives and hearts. Those who follow the path of righteousness will find joy and contentment in this world and after death, but those who are evil will perish.

Understanding the Gathas

The language in which the older portions of the Avesta is written, Gathic Avestan, is the only known example of this particular dialect. It survived in the oral tradition through centuries because people believed that the sounds of the Gathic words were especially pleasing to Ahura Mazda. Because of its great age and obscure dialect, the Avesta is notoriously difficult to translate and to understand. Gathic words often had a number of meanings. Many different interpretations are possible, even likely. For example, *Sraosha* is the name of an angel or a characteristic of

Ahura Mazda, but may also mean "conscience" or "obedience." Much depends on context and the skill of the translator.

Zoroastrian scholars continually debate the exact meanings of different passages. Zarathushtra was preaching to people who understood not only his language but references to the Iranian gods and religious practices. As in all poetry, the language may be compressed and the meaning difficult to interpret. Zarathushtis may spend their whole lives trying to understand what Zarathushtra meant. But for them, the challenge of understanding is one of the things that keeps their religion fresh and alive.

The Visperad

This part of the Avesta is a long liturgical text that is based on the Yasna and Vendidad, a priestly code, with additional invocations. It is used to celebrate the great holy days, or gahambars, of Zoroastrianism.

The Yashts

The Yashts are twenty-one hymns of praise to yazatas—angels and other divine beings. They are composed in Young Avestan, indicating that they came into the literature after the Yasna, but their content goes back to a much earlier time. Many Yashts praise earlier gods and goddesses of nature, such as Mithra, a deity of ancient Iran, who reappears in Zoroastrianism as the deity of Heavenly Light. Another being praised in the Yashts is Sraosha, the first of the heavenly beings to worship Ahura Mazda and later one of the deities to help the faithful across the Chinvat Bridge, along with Mithra and Rashnu, the spirit of Justice. Other Yashts praise such spirits as Conscience, Victory, the Wind, Sun, and Rain, Righteousness, the haoma plant, and the geographical features of the Iranian world. There are also hymns to the fravashis, the guardian spirits of all living beings. The Hormazd Yasht lists the seventy-two names of Ahura Mazda, "the sustainer, maintainer, creator and nourisher," which may be recited to guard against evil.

The Yashts suggest a time when Zoroastrianism was incorporating elements of the old Iranian religion. In praising such deities as the Wind, Victory, and the Rain Star, they connect Zoroastrianism to the ancient Iranian religion before Zarathushtra.

The Vendidad

The Vendidad contains the priestly code of Zoroastrianism. It is mainly concerned with ritual and physical purity. It is not certain whether Zarathushtra himself laid down rules for purity, but spiritual purity was important in his teaching. In order to be spiritually pure, one had to be physically pure. This meant respecting the elements of fire, water, air, and earth; maintaining personal cleanliness; and avoiding pollution. The most serious form of pollution was that of coming in contact with death, and the Vendidad presents rules for purifying those who handle the dead. Purification rites help to keep away the forces of evil. There are also remedies for offenses such as causing physical harm to another person or a good animal.

The early chapters of the Vendidad do not deal with ritual purity. The first tells how Ahura Mazda creates sixteen happy lands, only to have them attacked by Angra Mainyu. The second tells how the Aryan (Iranian) people traveled south, into Iran, in search of grazing land for their animals. Chapter 3 describes the joy of the earth when righteous people settle and plant crops upon it, and its sorrow when evil attacks. People are urged to undo evil to please the earth.

Minor Texts of the Avesta

This section of the Avesta contains the Nyayesh and the Gah. These are prayers recited during the regular prayer cycle by both priests and laypeople. The five Nyayesh are addressed to the Sun and Moon, as symbols of Ahura Mazda; to Mithra, the spirit of Light, and to Water and Fire. The five Gah are similar. Each day is divided into five gah, or periods, for prayer. The Gah are prayers Zarathushtis recite five times each day. Both the Nyayesh and the Gah contain invocations and passages from the Gathas and the Yashts.

Another text in this section is the Khorda Avesta or "Little Avesta." It combines sections from the other texts in the Avesta, both in Avestan and the later Middle Persian, or Pahlavi, lan-

■ The Names of Ahura Mazda

From a litany from the Hormazad Yasht of the Avesta

I am the sustainer, maintainer, and the reformer of my creations.

I am both the creator and nourisher [thereof],
  and I am possessed of the faculty of premonition.

I am the most bountiful spirit,

I am the giver of the greatest blessings of good health,
  through my name,

I am the most perfect giver of the greatest good health,
  through my name,

I am by name Athravan [the keeper of the sacred flame],

I am by name the most perfect Athravan,

I am by name Ahura, the creator of life,

I am by name Mazda, the omniscient,

I am by name holy righteousness,

I am by name the possessor of the highest degree of
  divine righteousness,

I am by name, glory,

By name I am the holder of the greatest glory,

I am by name, a complete seer,

I am by name the most complete seer,

By [my] name, "I Exist,"...

I am by name the provider of bounties,

I am by name the master-thought, that provides bounties,

I am by name the wielder of divine power, glory and will,

I am by name the glorious wielder of divine authority,...

I am by name the one opposed to destructiveness
  and wickedness,

I am by name the one who overcomes opposition of evil,

I am by name the one who overcomes all manner
  of obstacles,

I am by name the fashioner of all creations,

I am by name illimitable radiance,

I am by name the complete distributor of my universal radiance.

I am by name the unextinguishable light of the universe.

—*Daily Prayers of the Zoroastrians*, transl. Framroz Rustomjee guages. This combined text is a prayer book for everyday use by Zarathushtis. All copies of the Khorda Avesta contain the same basic materials, but sometimes in different order. Some also include prayers in a more modern language, such as Persian or Gujarati. The Khorda Avesta first came into popular use in the nineteenth century, when the holy texts became widely available.

Fragments of the Avesta

The Great Avesta of the Sasanian era contained not only the sacred Avestan scriptures, but also many other texts. It included stories and legends of the Prophet's life from oral sources, books of Zoroastrian law, tales of creation and the end of the world, and all that was known of science, astronomy, and the universe at the time. All copies of this huge work were lost in the Arab invasion and later invasions by the Turks and the Mongols. Fragments of the Great Avesta that did survive have been collected into a small section of today's Avesta.

The Pahlavi Zand

The Avesta of today is sometimes called the Zand (or Zend) Avesta or the Avesta-Zand. The word *zand* refers to explanations, commentaries, and translations. Commentary was probably always a part of the Avesta, but the earliest notes have been lost. The Zand, written in Pahlavi, comes down to us from Sasanian times. The Sasanians produced a great body of Zand. Scholar-priests continued to research and write for a long time after the Arab invasion, well into the ninth century. One of the later texts is the *Denkard*, which summarizes the contents of the Avesta from beginning to end.

The Zand is often the only clue to what the Avesta included before wars and invasions destroyed it. It is immensely helpful in reconstructing Avestan history and in showing how the Avesta has been interpreted and explained over many centuries.

The Bundahishn

One part of the Lost Avesta that appears in the Zand is the *Bundahishn,* or "Creation." The Bundahishn tells the story of the creation of the world. Ahura Mazda created the first man,

Gayomart. From him came the first couple, from whom came the races of humankind. When they assumed human form, Ahura Mazda taught them the principles of the Mazdayazni religion, the forerunner of Zoroastrianism: *think good thoughts, speak good words, do good deeds, and do not worship the demons* (G.Bd. 14.11). The story of creation, like the other myths and legends of pre-history that appear in the Zand with ritual and historical fact, is an important link in a continuous chain of truth in the consciousness of Zarathushti people.

The book also tells the nature of the divine beings, the Amesha Spentas, and details the end of the world. According to the Bundahishn, at the end of time, the earth will be covered with molten metal. The wise and just, led by their Savior, will walk through the metal as if it were warm milk, while the evil will be consumed in it. When the earth has been purified by fire, all the dead will rise and live in peace and harmony in Ahura Mazda's perfected world.

The Importance of the Avesta

The Avesta is one of the world's oldest scriptures. Its blend of ritual and inspiration contains all that Zarathushtis have needed to follow their faith and live according to its precepts for over three thousand years. Although it has come down to us only in part, it speaks to people in modern times much as it did in Zarathushtra's day. It remains the essential guide to the "Good Religion" that Zarathushtis rely on in their devotions and in their daily lives.

There are also some non-Zoroastrian writings that could serve as sources for the study of its teachings. These are the inscriptions dating from the time of the Persian kings Cyrus and Darius that speak of a god Ahuramazda. However, the Zoroastrian orthodoxy of these inscriptions has been challenged. The reason it has been challenged is because Cyrus's mausoleum indicates entombment, which was not in keeping with the Zoroastrian customs. These other writings, then, seem more appropriate for studying the history and development of Zoroastrianism rather than helping us to understand the message of its religious founder.

CHAPTER **6**

Philosophy and Ethics in Zoroastrianism

Zoroastrianism, like many religions, provides its followers with a philosophy, or guidelines by which to live. A deeply ethical religion, it leads them to make moral choices. Zarathushtra's great vision for humankind was to see people as capable of rational thought and fundamentally ethical—that is, able to make right decisions about how they live their lives. For a Zarathushti, the most important religious duty is to lead a moral life.

In Zarathushtra's view, life is a series of choices between good and evil. He urged his followers to choose goodness. Zoroastrians are taught to strive always to follow the path of Asha, or Truth. To be Zarathushti is to respect and honor such virtues as truth, kindness, humility, compassion, gratitude, love of family and friends, respect for others and for the community, respect for the environment, kindness to animals, hard work, hospitality, and generosity. These are the "Good Thoughts, Good Words, and Good Deeds" of Zoroastrianism.

Following the Amesha Spentas

The Amesha Spentas provide a framework for living the good life that Zarathushtra described. They are aspects of Ahura

Mazda himself, which later became personified as spirits or angels. By focusing on the virtues represented by the Amesha Spentas, humans may acquire these virtues themselves. The Amesha Spentas thus provide a framework for Zarathushti life.

Asha, the Path of Truth

Asha is a Gathic word and difficult to translate. The closest we can come to it in English is "truth" and "righteousness," but Asha means more than that. It carries with it the idea of perfection. Asha is truth, wisdom, righteousness, justice, and progress in one ideal. In Zoroastrian belief, there is no higher ideal than Asha. The perfect world of Ahura Mazda is organized according to Asha, the ideal Truth. Zarathushtis try to follow the path of Asha in their lives.

Of all the principles laid down in the Gathas by Zarathushtra, Asha is perhaps the most important. Zarathushtra mentions it more than any other principle, and he obviously considered it essential to the practice of Zoroastrianism. He says, "For as long as I am able, and have any strength, I shall pursue the Truth [Asha]" (Ys. 28.4). The importance of Asha goes beyond the Gathas. The *Ashem Vohu,* which is considered to be the most basic prayer of Zoroastrianism, praises Asha above all things. The entire Yasna, the part of the Avesta that contains the main liturgy and prayers of Zoroastrianism, ends, "There is but one path, that of Asha; all other paths are false paths." Therefore, in order to be Zoroastrian, men and women must practice the principle of Asha in their daily lives. That means that they must try sincerely to pursue the Truth and to live according to it.

Pursuing the truth has never been easy. There may be many truths, although what someone believes is not necessarily true, no matter how sincerely he or she believes it. There are different kinds of truth—for example, spiritual truth and scientific truth. Truth is difficult to know. Moreover, we are limited in our ability to know it by our human viewpoint.

Zarathushtis know that they may pursue Asha for a lifetime and never fully know it. But they must never stop trying to learn it and act according to it. This means constantly searching, constantly learning, constantly questioning, and constantly listening—to other Zarathushtis, to their own conscience, to the words of Zarathushtra.

The Good Mind

To help people know and follow the path of Asha, Ahura Mazda has given them Vohu Mana, the Good Mind. Like Asha, this is an aspect of Ahura Mazda that people may aspire to cultivate in their own lives. From the Good Mind of Zoroastrianism come Good Thoughts, and from Good Thoughts follow Good Words and Good Deeds. The Good Mind helps people to choose what is true and valuable in life.

People are not born with Vohu Mana. Indeed, learning to be in touch with the Good Mind is a lifelong process. The Good Mind develops through thoughtful study and through being mindful of and practicing goodness. To be always truthful, kind, cheerful, and faithful is a demanding discipline, although it grows easier with practice. Temptation towards evil is always with us. People must work at not abusing such things as wine and sexuality, at being humble and avoiding egotism, at not giving in to laziness and pessimism. In Zoroastrianism, it is not enough to refrain from doing evil just because one fears punishment. Evil thoughts are evil. To think evil is to take a step toward doing it. Zarathushtis try always to turn their minds toward

A Faravahar symbol adorns the entrance of a modern Darbe Mehr.

righteousness and goodness. They must continually ask themselves, "What is good?" and "What is True?" Moreover, it is not enough to be good oneself but to tolerate evils and ignorance in society or in others. It is necessary to actively fight evil wherever one finds it.

The human capacity to think carries with it the responsibility to use the product of thought to make right choices. Zarathushtis choose truth and goodness through their free will. This gift of Ahura Mazda enables them to decide whether they will follow the path of goodness and righteousness, or act in ways that are ignorant, sinful, and evil. No one is there to guide them but the goodness that they cultivate within themselves. There is no personal savior, as in Christianity, and no amount of faith will save someone who has chosen the evil path. Zarathushtis must choose right because it is right and for no other reason. Choice is deeply important in Zoroastrianism: at their Navjote and in daily prayers ever after, Zarathushtis affirm that they have chosen their religion and to follow the preachings of the prophet Zarathushtra.

Armaity

Spenta Armaity is the spirit of Generosity and Love. It is the aspect of Ahura Mazda that inspires people to reach out to others. The world is not just spiritual and physical, but also social. It is organized into families, associations, workplaces, churches, towns and cities, nations. People have to learn to get along. This does not imply weakness, because Zoroastrians are quick to fight for what they believe to be right. But they try to work through persuasion and example, not force.

There are evils in the social world, such as hunger, poverty, warfare, and strife. It is through Armaity that people commit themselves to love, to help the poor, to work for peace. The spirit of Armaity helps people to perform the acts of charity and kindness that will eventually bring about Ahura Mazda's perfect world.

Khshathra Vairya: Just Dominion

People who make their own lives rich and pure through following good thoughts, good words, and good deeds find the power of Ahura Mazda within themselves. Khshathra Vairya is not leadership by worldly might, but by moral force. Those who acquire it are leaders within their families, within their communities, and out in the world as they work to create a better society. The potential for developing this aspect of Ahura Mazda is within everyone, but achieving the power conferred by Ahura Mazda may take a lifetime.

Haurvatat and Ameratat

Completeness and Immortality go together. When a Zoroastrian has achieved righteousness and completeness in this life, he or she may hope to achieve Ameratat, or Immortality.

Dualism

Zoroastrianism is sometimes described as being based on *dualism*. This is the belief that good and evil are two equal and opposing forces that balance the universe. Zarathushtra himself introduced the notion of opposing forces, Truth and the Lie, in

■ Portrait of the prophet Zarathushtra.

the Gathas. In referring to these forces, he used the word *mainyu*, which can mean both "spirit" and "mentality." He called them "twins" (Ys. 30) and said that they "never agree."

Zoroastrians have often debated just what Zarathushtra meant when he described these forces. Were they both the creations of Ahura Mazda? Did they already exist in the universe before creation? Or do they exist only within the human heart and mind? The Gathas do not really say. Did Zarathushtra mean spirits of the sort to which the human mind can give shape and character? Or was he creating a metaphor about our mentalities, the spirit within us? Zoroastrians and historians cannot agree on the interpretation. In the history of Zoroastrianism, scholars have tended to see Angra Mainyu, or Ahriman, the Spirit of the Lie, as a universal force and cast him as the leader of the forces of evil. This way of looking at the two forces is called *cosmic dualism.* Later thinkers interpret the Gathas as saying that evil is the product of the choices people make in their lives. This view is called *ethical dualism.* Although these two views differ, they are

| ■ The Amesha Spentas | | | |
Name	Meaning	Creation Protected	How represented in ritual
Spenta Mainyu	Holy spirit	humankind	the priest
Vohu Mana	Good Mind	animals	milk
Asha	Best righteousness	fire	ritual flame
Armaity	Holy devotion	earth	holy space
Khshathra Vairya	Wise dominion	sky	stone mortar and pestle
Haurvatat	Wholeness	water	consecrated water
Ameretat	Immortality	plants	Haoma and other plants, flowers

not so very far apart. Both agree that good and evil exist and that evil must be conquered.

Zarathushtra gave us the dual principles of Truth and the Lie—Spenta Mainyu and Angra Mainyu, or Ahriman. He set up the battle between good and evil, but he did not see them as equal. Ahriman is powerful, but in the end, Ahura Mazda will prevail. Eventually, people will give their lives to following his path, the path of Asha.

Good and Evil in Zoroastrian Belief

The idea of dualism is the way Zarathushtra answered the question that has plagued believers of many religions throughout history. How do we explain the existence of evil in the world? Why doesn't a good and all-powerful God simply do away with evil, ignorance, and injustice?

According to Zoroastrian belief, Ahura Mazda created the world in two stages. The first was the spiritual, or *Menog,* stage. Ahura Mazda created the fravashis (guardian spirits) of all living things. All things, including human life, had no physical form. Everything was pure and without evil. Ahura Mazda asked the fravashis if he should give them physical form. He warned that if he did so, they would no longer be perfect. Evil would enter the creation. If it did so, they would have to fight a long and hard battle to defeat it. The fravashis, however, wanted physical bodies. With physical form, they would be free to act, rather than remain forever in a state of inaction. In return for physical being, they would fight Evil.

Ahura Mazda brought the physical, or *Getig,* world into being. As he had warned, with it came evil, in the form of Angra Mainyu, or Ahriman, who would bring imperfection, sin, evil, and death into the world. Ahura Mazda then set the holy spirit, Spenta Mainyu, the Truth, to guide the fravashis and to lead the battle against Angra Mainyu, the Lie.

With the twin spirits, Truth and the Lie, the world entered a stage called *Gumeisn,* the Mixture. This is the stage in which we now live. Good and Bad, Truth and the Lie, both exist in the universe. These two can never agree, and so they must fight each other for the souls of humankind. Humans must fight evil in their

■ *Two young boys in training for the priesthood in Andheri, a suburb of Bombay. They are practicing the preliminary ceremony for the great rite of the Yasna. The boy in the role of officiating priest sits cross-legged before the sacred fire, while his assistant stands nearby.*

hearts and minds. This they do with the help of Spenta Mainyu, the holy spirit of Ahura Mazda, and the Beneficent Immortals.

By living ethical lives and following the path of Asha, people participate in the battle against Ahriman. Their good actions help to bring about the destruction of evil. Toward the end of this time, three Saviors will be born one thousand years apart. They will lead the righteous in the final battle against evil.

Saoshyants

The term "saoshyant" (savior) was applied to Zoroaster's followers because he believed that the apocalypse was imminent. There was urgency to his efforts to gather as many followers as he could to fight and conquer the hostile spirit and usher in the frosokereti. He pleaded, "May we be those who make existence brilliant." When the apocalypse did not come immediately, the saoshyant was no longer viewed as a general portrait of all those who worked toward "the end." The saoshyant was transformed into a particular figure who would bring about "the end." Eventually, the vision of the saoshyant focused on three successive saoshyants, separated by thousands of years. They would usher in eras of peace after the forces of evil seemed to prevail. The appearance of the first of these saviors would mark the decline of the trend toward evil and a reversal to a time of justice, peace, and piety.

Frashogard

In time, all people die, but their fravashis and their souls are immortal. Where their souls exist in the afterlife reflects the choices they made during life. All their thoughts, words, and deeds in their lifetime become part of their soul. Those who have sincerely followed the path of Asha may pass confidently into the Abode of Songs, or heaven. The others fall into the abyss of hell.

In Zoroastrian thought, however, hell is not permanent. It exists only until, as will surely happen, good overcomes evil. Then the dead will rise, purified and redeemed. Even Ahriman will repent and return to the worship of Ahura Mazda.

This time, toward which all Zarathushtis work through their good deeds and through living moral and ethical lives, is Frashogard or Frashokereti, which means "renewal" or "freshening." The physical and spiritual worlds will be united in a perfect, Menog stage. All creation will exist forever in a state of perfection.

CHAPTER 7

Rituals and Rites of Passage

*L*ike most religions, Zoroastrianism has many meaningful rituals. The origins of these, such as the Yasna, stretch back into prehistory. They probably come from Iranian religious custom in the time before Zarathushtra. In Zoroastrianism, priests perform the religion's highly prescribed rituals in consecrated temples at regular intervals throughout the day. These rituals are closed to all but confirmed members of the faith who are in a state of ritual purity. Those who qualify may attend, although there is no requirement to do so. The basic rituals consist of caring for the consecrated fire; performing the Yasna rituals; and purifying those who have come in contact with pollution. The priests may also offer prayers and special rituals for individuals who request them.

Except for the Vendidad, which is read aloud by a priest, the priests memorize all the rituals. The language of the ritual is Avestan, which is believed to be especially pleasing to the ear of Ahura Mazda. Traditionally, the basic ritual of the Yasna has been the haoma ritual, in which priests ritually extract juice from the haoma plant as an offering.

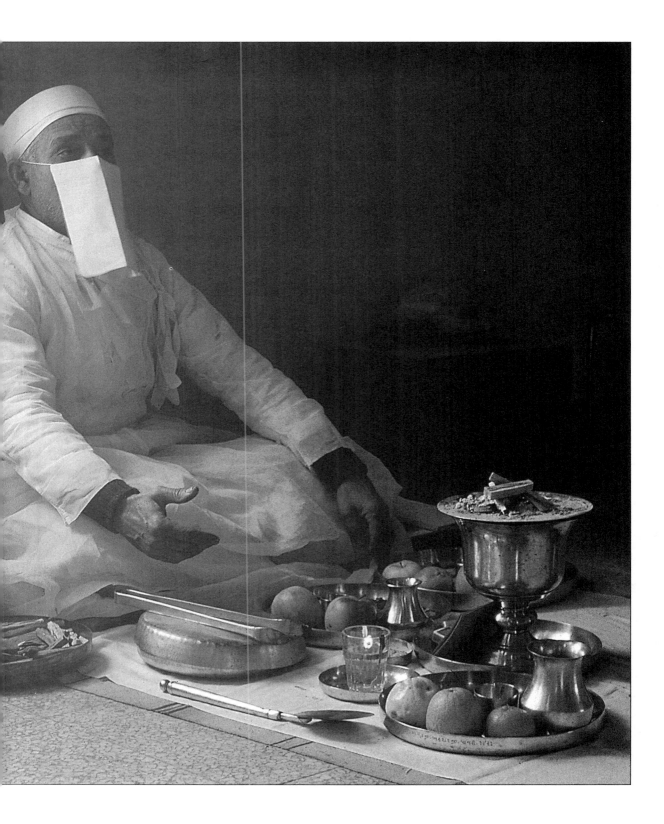

The highest rituals of Zoroastrianism may be carried out only in the presence of consecrated fire, which is kept only in a fire temple built with specially consecrated tools and consecrated with a series of rituals. In North America and other countries around the world, there is no consecrated temple or consecrated fire. People send their special prayer requests to the high priests in India or Iran, where the holiest of ceremonies are celebrated.

Keeping the Sacred Fire

Zoroastrian tradition says that the great fires of their religion have been burning since prehistory. The first fire is said to have been brought from heaven on the back of the mythical ox, Srishok, to be the guide and protector of humankind for all time. Fire represents the spiritual rule of light over darkness and is the sacred symbol of Ahura Mazda.

Behram fire is the most powerful of all temple fires. It protects against the powers of darkness and does battle with the Lie. In the Atash Behram, the fire rests on a platform over which is a crown that represents its sovereignty. The Behram fire is made up of fires gathered from sixteen different sources specified in the Avesta. One source must be fire ignited by lightning, which comes directly from Ahura Mazda; others are consecrated fires from other temples. The rituals for purifying a fire are performed 1,128 times, a process that takes a year. The most sacred fires of Zoroastrianism reside in consecrated temples in Iran and India. They have been burning continuously for centuries. The fires of India were carried overland from Iran in medieval times by Zarathushtis who fled Muslim persecution.

The Boi Ceremony

The ceremony that accompanies the regular tending of the fire five times a day is called *Boi-Machi*. The fire is usually fed with sandalwood, which has a sweet odor when burned; worshipers may purchase it at the temple and donate it as an offering. In an Atash Behram, the highest grade of fire temple, it is tended by white-gloved priests who have undergone the most rigorous purification.

■ The Zoroastrian Calendars

The Zoroastrians of Persia had a calendar of twelve thirty-day months, or 360 days. They added five special "Gatha Days" to bring the calendar closer to the actual 365-day year. Instead of adding a day every four years to account for the extra one-quarter day each year, as we do, they added a month every 120 years to bring the months back into line with the seasons. At some point, however, they stopped adding the extra month. Their calendar was called Qadmi or Kadmi.

The Parsis took the Persian calendar to India with them. They continued to add the extra month, and so their calendar came to differ from the Qadmi calendar. In 1720, a priest visiting from Iran noticed that the Iranians and the Parsis were using different calendars. Some returned to the Qadmi calendar used by the Iranians. Others stayed with their calendar, called Shenshai. To try to reconcile the two, a scholar recommended using a more modern calendar of 365 and one-quarter days. That way the spring equinox (the date when night and day are the same length) always falls on March 21. Those who adopted this calendar called it Fasli for "following the seasons."

As a result, there are three different Zoroastrian calendars, and different groups of Zoroastrians celebrate their gahambars at different times of the year. On the Fasli calendar, NoRoz always falls on March 21, but on the Qadmi or Shenshai calendars, it may fall in July or August.

The priest prays the appropriate prayers and then places six pieces of sandalwood (or other dry wood in the shape of a throne) and frankincense, a spice, over the fire. Then the wood is placed in the fire urn, or *afargan*. The priest, carrying a metal ladle, then circles the fire, stopping eight times to repeat a prayer in Avestan, which means the following:

> O Ahura Mazda, we praise Thee through Thy visible
> symbol, the fire. We praise Thee by our offering of
> Good thoughts, words, and deeds.

The priest then strikes a bell, symbolically calling the holy spirit to be present in the room. After the ceremony, the priest uses the ladle to give ash from the fire to any worshipers who are present.

The Priesthood

The Zoroastrian priesthood has traditionally been hereditary in the male line, although now in Iran, men may qualify through study. The duties of priests include reciting the liturgy in the temples and in the homes of members of the community, saying prayers for the dead, and conducting weddings, Navjotes, and Jashans. Zoroastrian priests are known as Mobeds; in India, they are called Dasturs. There are several levels in the priestly hierarchy. The highest grade of priest is known as a *Mobed e Mobedan,* or *Dasturja Dasturan.* Mobedyars are priests in training.

In India, priestly training usually begins when boys are in their early to mid-teens. It requires memorizing the basic scriptures and liturgy and undergoing a series of purification rituals. The basic liturgy, the Yasna, is always recited in Avestan, so memorization is by rote. The candidate spends a period of nine days in retreat and undergoes a second purification ritual. Then he is dressed in white, the color of purity, and ordained by a senior Mobed. After the ritual, he recites the Yasna. Over the following days, he recites other liturgies, earning the right to be called *Ervad*. He may perform basic ceremonies, including the Navjote and wedding ceremonies, although he may not celebrate high rituals, including the Yasna. Many young men stop at this level and go into other professions.

If he is to continue, the young priest then spends the next two to three years learning additional scriptures before undergoing further purification rituals and becoming a full Mobed. When he has demonstrated a mastery of all the rituals, he is qualified to perform any Zoroastrian ceremony. As a rule, candidates for the priesthood learn the rituals by memorization and practice. They are not expected to learn Avestan and Pahlavi, although they may take lessons in the meaning of the rituals through translation. If they attend college later, they may study the languages of Zoroastrianism at that time.

The examination for the priesthood in Iran is similar, but candidates are tested more intensively on their knowledge and understanding of the religion, and there is only one grade of priest. The new Mobed practices with others for a year, after which he is on his own.

The Holy Days of Zoroastrianism

Zoroastrians do not gather weekly for regular worship services. Instead, they recite the basic daily prayers five times daily, either alone, in informal groups, or as a family. They do, however, have holidays or festivals during which they join together for worship and celebration.

There are seven great Zoroastrian festivals each year. Ancient in origin, they are linked to the Iranian agricultural year and to the seven physical creations for which the Amesha Spentas are responsible. In the Atash Behrams, priests recite the holy day's special liturgy. People participate in the Jashan, or thanksgiving and memorial ceremony, and follow the special custom of the day, which may be merrymaking, putting on new clothes, or visiting the fire temple. The holy days are times when the entire community, both rich and poor, comes together to share a feast, to which everyone contributes according to their

Seven Holy Days of Zoroastrianism			
The Gahambars:			
English Name	Amesha Spenta	Associated Creation	Time of Year*
Midspring	Khshathra	Sky	April/May
Midsummer	Haurvatat	Water	June/July
Bringing in Corn	Spenta Armaity	Earth	September
Homecoming	Ameratat	Plants	October
Midwinter	Vohu Mana	Cattle	January
All Souls	Spenta Mainyu/ Ahura Mazda	Humankind	March
New Year (NoRoz)	Asha Vahista	Fire	March

*These are the approximate times according to the ancient and present Zoroastrian Fasli calendar.

ability. In ancient times, a ruler might bring barrels of wine and whole roasted animals, and a poor man bring a single onion, but all contribute to the joy and merriment of the occasion.

The six Zoroastrian gahambars are:

- *Maidhyoizaremaya* (Midspring)
- *Maidhyoishema* (Midsummer)
- *Paitshahya* (Harvest)
- *Ayathrima* (Bringing in Cattle)
- *Maidhyairya* (Midwinter)
- *Hamaspathmaedaya, Muktad* (All Souls)

The seventh and highest festival is NoRoz, the New Year. The festival celebrates the creation of fire and the Beneficent Immortal Asha Vahista, or Highest Truth. It is thus the most sacred and joyous of all Zoroastrian holy days. It is held in the spring, just after the sixth gahambar, and so represents the renewal of life that spring symbolizes. It also represents the new order to come with Frashogard, world renewal. On NoRoz, people exchange presents, put on new clothes, settle any outstanding arguments, and visit their fire temple to reaffirm their faith.

Zoroastrians celebrate gahambars as part of their religious duty. They believe that such times of community joy and harmony provide a glimpse of the spiritual world.

■ *Iranian women pre-pare the table for the celebration of NoRoz, or the New Year.*

Jashan: The Thanksgiving and Memorial Ceremony

Jashan is a ceremony for thanksgiving and memorializing. It is performed during the gahambars and NoRoz, the New Year, but it may be performed at any time that people want to express gratitude and happiness, as for a wedding, a Navjote, a house-warming, or the dedication of a new Darbe Mehr. Individuals may also sponsor a Jashan for a celebration, or in memory of someone who has died.

The Jashan requires at least two priests, who take the parts of the Zaotar (speaker) and the Raspi (assistant), but often four participate. The ceremony represents a dialogue between the spiritual and the physical worlds, symbolically linking the two. It invites Ahura Mazda, the Amesha Spentas, the yazatas, and the fravashis and souls of the dead to join in.

The priests sit on the floor on either side of a cloth that contains an afargan, or fire urn, a tray of sandalwood and incense for feeding the fire, and a tray of offerings of flowers, fruit, milk, and bread and frequently wine. They begin by lighting the fire and offering prayers to consecrate it. They then remember the departed souls of the faithful, starting with Zarathushtra and Zoroastrian heroes. They first repeat prayers related to the person or event being celebrated or remembered. In the next part of the Jashan, the flowers on the tray before them are exchanged during the recitation of a prayer. The exchange of flowers symbolizes the journey of the fravashis from heaven to the earthly world and back. They repeat the yatha ahu vairyo and Ashem vohu prayers and the prayers of thanksgiving. The priest calls on the spiritual world to bless the worshipers, reciting a special prayer, the *afringan,* for those who sponsored the Jashan. The ceremony is then at an end.

The ceremony is an expression of happiness: gratitude for past blessings and joy in the good things in the present and future. The Jashan is always accompanied by a feast in which all members of the community participate.

Zoroastrians celebrate other thanksgiving days as well. These include the dates of the Prophet's birth and death and days that recall the yazatas, such as the divinity of Rain and Fertility, the divinity of Water, and Mithra, the divinity of Sun and Justice. They also celebrate the five Gatha days at the end of the year by remembering the fravashis of those who have died and giving thanks for those in the present world whom they love and care for.

Navjote

The ceremony in which young people are initiated into Zoroastrianism is known as *Navjote.* Among Iranian Zoroastrians, the age for Navjote, or as it is called there, Sudre-Pushti, has traditionally been fifteen. Parsi Zarathushtis perform it at an earlier age, usually seven or nine, but no later than eleven. The Navjote is a coming-of-age ceremony for young people who are considered mature enough to understand and uphold the principles of the faith. Before they can be initiated, they must learn the ways of Zarathushtra and what it means to be a Zoroastrian. This training, which begins in babyhood, is the responsibility of their parents. With the Navjote, young people take on the responsibility for their own lives by choosing good over evil. From that time on, their parents are no longer responsible for their actions. The Navjote is the same for both boys and girls.

At the Navjote, the initiate receives the symbols of the religion. These are the *sudreh* and the *kusti.* The sudreh is a white muslin garment ceremonially made, which devout Zoroastrians wear as an undergarment. It symbolizes purity. The kusti is a cord that is wrapped around the body. It is woven from lamb's wool and symbolizes Vohu Mana, the Good Mind. Besides being a reminder that the wearer is bound to the Good Religion, the kusti plays an important part in Zoroastrian daily prayer and ritual.

The initiate comes to the Navjote freshly bathed. Before the ceremony begins, the young person recites special prayers, including the Kusti prayers that are part of daily worship. He or she is then asked to sip a consecrated liquid. Traditionally, this has been *nirang*, bull's urine that has been ritually prepared, although pomegranate juice is often used today. The drink ritually cleanses the body and soul within. Then the initiate recites a series of prayers, including the Ashem Vohu, the "Principle of Righteousness," in a prescribed order. He or she then goes for a ritual bath, or *Nahan*. These actions symbolize inner and outer purification.

After the Nahan, the initiate returns to the room where the ceremony will be held, dressed entirely in white and wearing the white cap that Zoroastrians always wear during prayer. The officiating priest recites the *Patet*, or "repentance," prayer, which represents a turning away from sin. After that, the initiate and the priest stand facing each other, holding the sudreh together. Together, they recite the *Din No Kalmo*, or "Declaration of Faith." Next, the priest puts the sudreh on the initiate. In taking the sudreh, the initiate symbolically accepts the responsibility of working for good and helping to bring about the final renovation of the world.

The priest then stands behind the initiate and ties on the kusti according to prescribed ritual, while the two pray aloud together. The kusti is circled around the initiate's waist three times and knotted four times. The three circles around the waist represent Good Thoughts, Good Words, and Good Deeds. The exact symbolic meaning of the knots is not known, but one explanation is that the first represents one God, the second that Zoroastrianism is the word of God, the third that Zarathushtra is the Prophet of God, and the fourth is a reminder that the wearer is bound to the religion forever. Zarathushtis are to wear the kusti at all times, tying and untying it and reciting the basic prayers and according to tradition on getting up, after using the bathroom, before daily prayers, after a bath, and before meals.

After receiving the sudreh and kusti, as a necessary part of the ritual, the initiate recites a declaration of his or her faith in Ahura Mazda. The priest—or priests, if more than one is attending—offers a final blessing, completing the ceremony. The young person is now a full member of the Zoroastrian faith.

Weddings

Zoroastrians are expected to marry and produce children, the only way in which Zoroastrianism can grow and prosper. The participants all wear white, the color worn by Zoroastrians on religious occasions. Traditionally, Zoroastrian weddings are held at home, although hotels and other meeting places may be used. The groom often enters in a procession of musicians and guests, led by a priest. At least two priests lead the ceremony. The couple sit next to each other, with witnesses, usually members of each family, behind them. Like all Zoroastrian ceremonies, the wedding takes place in the presence of a fire.

The ceremony begins with a benediction. The senior priest expresses the hope that the couple will have long lives, lasting love, health and strength, and be blessed with children and grandchildren. The priest then asks the witnesses if they agree to

A dakhma, or tower of silence, the traditional place of disposal of the dead, stands on an Iranian hilltop outside the town of Yazd.

the union and, when the answer is yes, asks the couple if they have agreed "with a righteous mind" to be married until the end of their lives. Each replies individually, "We have agreed." The ceremony recalls the wedding of Pouruchista and Jamaspa, during which Zarathushtra asked his daughter if she freely agreed to the marriage.

Priests and witnesses may pass a long string around the couple, symbolically binding them together, and then offer prayers and blessings. The couple are showered with rice, symbolic of prosperity and joy.

Funerals

In Zoroastrian tradition, death represents the strongest form of ritual impurity or pollution. Therefore, Zoroastrians have strict rituals associated with death and dying. These rituals begin even before death. If a person is known to be dying, family members bring a fire into the room to drive away evil.

According to Zoroastrian belief, the evil spirit of decay rushes into the body within three hours after death. Because of the extreme pollution of death, no one may touch the dead except special "corpse bearers" who are especially trained, and who undergo special purification rituals after their work is done. Anyone else who touches the body must undergo ritual purification, or Nahan. All of the rituals surrounding death stress that the living should avoid the pollution of death.

The corpse bearers ritually wash the body and dress it in a clean sudreh and kusti. The body is shrouded, with only the face uncovered. They place the body on a stone slab and mark an area around the body into which the priests and family may not step. Fire fed with sandalwood and frankincense is kept burning beside the body to keep evil spirits away. A priest now comes and prays in Avestan. The priest is joined by at least one other for the *Geh Sarna* ceremony, in which they recite the first Gatha of Zarathushtra. The Geh Sarna ceremony signals the departure of the soul from the body. After the ceremony, the body is no longer connected to the soul and may be disposed of.

The members of the household say their goodbyes by looking on the body of the dead person, but without touching it. The corpse bearers then carry it out of the house on a metal bier (metal and stone do not absorb pollution, as wood does). Outside, the body is placed on a stone slab, and a dog is brought to look on the face of the dead person, a ceremony known as *Sagdid.* The dog both verifies death and drives away evil. Then the corpse bearers, followed by two priests and the mourners, carry the body to its final destination.

Towers of Silence

Since death is the ultimate victory of Ahriman over life, a dead body represents a state of extreme pollution. It should not

■ *Plan of a* dakhma, *or tower of silence. The structure is open to the sky. Dead bodies are placed on stone slabs: men on the outer ring, women in the middle, and children in the inner ring. Drains carry any matter not consumed by vultures away to a central well, which is sprinkled with acid from time to time for sanitation. Any remaining fragments are carried by drains to underground wells, where they return gradually to the earth.*

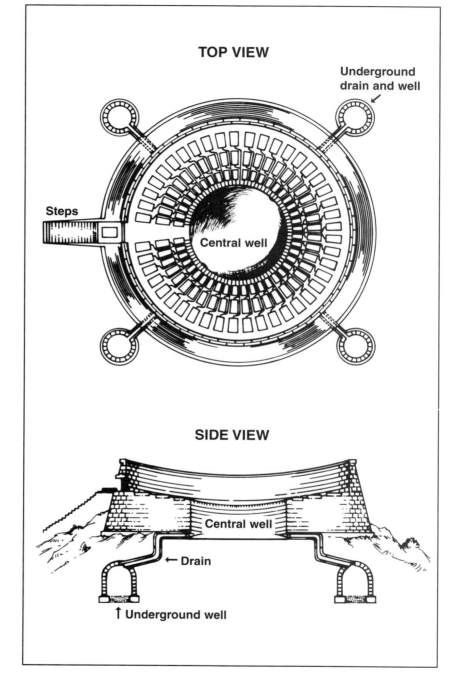

TOP VIEW

Underground drain and well

Steps

Central well

SIDE VIEW

Central well

← Drain

↑ Underground well

be allowed, therefore, to pollute the sacred elements: fire, water, air, or earth. The traditional way of disposing of a corpse in India and Iran has been the dakhma, or Tower of Silence. This is a circular stone building, open at the top, usually set on a barren hill. The inside is arranged in three circles. The outer circle is for men, the middle for women, and the inner circle for children.

Only corpse handlers may enter the building. They carry the body to the building, pause outside for mourners to say their last goodbyes, and then take the body inside and place it on a stone slab, where it is left to be devoured by vultures. The mourners withdraw to pray and then return home, where they pray and ritually bathe to cleanse themselves of the pollution of death. Throughout the following year, the family offers appropriate prayers for the dead.

In recent times, Zoroastrians have had to find other methods of disposing of their dead. Dakhmas are now in use mainly in parts of western India where the custom was established before the 1800s. The most traditional Zoroastrians around the world may return their dead to their home country, where they can be placed in a dakhma. Newer Parsi communities in India now have burial grounds, and Iranian Zoroastrians now use burial as well. Zoroastrians in other parts of the world may also use modern methods of cremation. Today's Zoroastrians reason that the prayers and rituals surrounding death are more important than the disposal of the body, so the least polluting method is considered appropriate.

Prayers for the Dead

At dawn on the third day, after death, the soul goes to meet the three judges, Mithra, Sraosha, and Rashnu. They judge the soul on its actions in life. It then passes on to the Chinvat Bridge, the Bridge of the Separator. There it meets its *Daena*, the guide who will take it across. She represents the person's conscience in life. If that life has been righteous, Daena is beautiful beyond all imagining and is accompanied by a sweet-smelling breeze. If the life has been one of ignorance and evil, the guide is an ugly hag with a foul odor.

The two move across the bridge. For the righteous, the bridge is wide and flat, and leads into eternal joy. For the wicked, it becomes narrower and narrower until it is a knife-blade, and the wicked soul falls off, into the pit of hell.

During this time, priests and the family continue with special prayers for the dead. Mourners may continue to recite the Patet, a prayer of repentance, and other prayers in honor and remembrance of the dead person daily for a month or even longer. Their prayers cannot, however, change the fate of the soul, which has been decided according to the dead person's behavior in life.

Excessive mourning is considered a sin in Zoroastrianism. It does not benefit the dead, and it harms the health of the living. Zoroastrianism teaches that the dead have moved on to eternal life and that in the final renovation of the world, all the dead will rise. People remember the dead, but their duty as Zoroastrians is to live fully in this world and be happy and optimistic. Feast days always include rituals for the dead, but as an occasion for joy, not sorrow.

Ritual and Belief in Zoroastrianism

Ritual, whether the high ritual of the Atash Behram or the Jashan gathering in a community hall, is an important part of Zoroastrianism. The rituals of Zoroastrianism carry the Zarathushti believer from birth to death, marking the important rites of passage and times of joy and sorrow, creating occasions for celebration and unity. In the ancient Zoroastrian rituals and prayers are all of the history of the faith and the poetry of the Gathas. The unbroken tradition of Zoroastrian ritual has helped to keep the religion strong and alive through more than three thousand years.

8

Zoroastrianism Facing the Future

$\boxed{A}$ generous estimate would admit that there are only about 150,000 Zoroastrians in the world today. Compared with Christians, Muslims, Hindus, and Buddhists, this is a very small number. Zoroastrianism is a religion that is local; it is a religion that began in ancient Persia (or modern Iran). Through Muslim persecution it became also a diaspora religion, spreading in 936 C.E., according to the traditional date, to India. More recently, due to the establishment of a Muslim Republic in Iran by the Ayattolah Khomeinei in 1979, many more Zoroastrians have fled their native land and migrated to Britain, Australia, Canada, and the United States. Zoroastrians, thus, now are not only small in numbers, but also a people who are dispersed. There are still strong communities of Zoroastrians in Iran and in India, where, despite the challenges of modern life and political difficulties, they hold to their traditions and adapt them to contemporary circumstances. Wherever they may be, however, Zoroastrians make efforts to keep their religious communities alive and active. Frequently, Zoroastrian communities sponsor social and religious events that promote their identity by supporting

■ *Baj (Prayer) for Grace Before Meals*

Ba name Yazad, bakhshayandeh bakshayashgar meherban!
    Hormazd Khodae itha at yazmaide,

Ahurem Mazdam, ye gamcha ashem-cha dat apascha dat
    urvaraoscha vanguish, raochaoscha dat bumimcha, vis-
    pacha vohu.

In the name of the Lord Ahura Mazda, bestower of all good things,
the generous spirited, and loving! Here we revere Ahura Mazda
who created the animals and grains, who created the waters
and vegetation, who created lights (of the sky), and the earth and
all good things.

Sinners. . .tyrants, wrongdoers and heretics, sinners, enemies and
witches! May they all be struck and defeated. . . .

—*Basic Daily Prayers of the Zoroastrians,* Framroz Rustomjee, 1959

lectures, adult discussion groups, and circles that study the Gathas. They also run instruction classes to teach the young about their religion and sponsor youth groups to bring together the bright hope of their future.

Zoroastrian Youth

Zoroastrianism today has two main strains: traditional Zoroastrianism and updated Zoroastrianism. The former is very much anchored in its Persian and Indian roots. In traditional Zoroastrianism, emphasis is placed on the identification of Zoroastrians as members of both a religious community and an ethnic group. This traditionalist view strongly recommends marriage only between Zoroastrians. The future of Zoroastrianism for these people is focused on the offspring of these unions: Zoroastrians beget Zoroastrians. In the vision of the traditional Zoroastrians, the young are the only future for the religion. On the other hand, updated Zoroastrianism has a different vision of the future. For proponents of updated Zoroastrians, Zoroastrianism is a religion, not an ethnic group. They believe that their religious future is not with the young alone, but also with converts from outside the ethnic circle. Still, each Zoroastrian group realizes the importance of youth for its future.

Both approaches to the religion make strong efforts to unite their young members through associations. One such association, the Zoroastrian Youth of North America (ZYNA), organizes activities for young people in the United States and Canada who are between the ages of 16 and 35. By means of summer camps and weekend retreats, this organization provides opportunities for young Zoroastrians to meet one another and to participate in discussions of their religious traditions. This association is cochaired by young people from Vancouver, British Columbia; New York; and Boston. Another association, under the umbrella of Zoroastrian Youth of North America, is the Zoroastrian Student Association at the University of Michigan, which sponsors forums and lectures for graduate and undergraduate students. Zoroastrians pay great attention to the young—from

■ *Dar-e Mehr on Mountain Hamilton in San Jose, California.*

those who are just beginning school all the way up to those who are finishing their professional degrees.

The Future of Zoroastrianism

Like many small religious communities, such as the Orthodox Jews, Zarathushtis wonder about their survival under modern pressures. The future seems particularly fragile among the Zarathushtis of the diaspora. There is such a limited number of the faithful and they are surrounded by cultures alien to their way of life and by religions that are better known and more affirmed by society. Ritual practices, which are so important for fostering and preserving community and so essential for traditionalists, often become watered down or even neglected in a diaspora world. Important religious reminders, such as the wearing of the sudreh and kusti, are often set aside (except for ceremonies) because some young believers wish to avoid standing out in a crowd. Because the priesthood is hereditary and there are so few sons of priests who want to continue in their fathers' footsteps in a world so distant from the world of traditional Zoroastrianism, continuance of worship becomes a problem. Also, Zoroastrian practices of burial are so foreign to those practiced in diaspora lands that it seems totally implausible that such rituals can be followed anywhere outside of Iran and India. The most sacred rituals—those that take place in an Atash Behram—cannot be transported to diaspora lands, as there is also no consecrated fire outside of Iran and India. The result is that Zoroastrians in the United States, Canada, Australia, and Great Britain are limited to celebrating festivals or having social events, forums, and lectures in Darbe Mehrs. None of these are fundamental Zoroastrian rituals. Most of the young in the diaspora worlds, then, have had no experience of a sacred ritual and have never entered an Atash Behram. The consequence of all of this ignorance is that these deeper aspects of their religion have little meaning for them.

Nevertheless, there are many efforts to nourish religious faith in spite of these limitations. Many modern Zarathushtis emphasize the ethical character of their religion more than the importance of ritual practices. They view the main teaching of

Zarathushtra as concerning itself with the discipline of good thoughts, good words, good deeds, and daily prayer.

> ■ **Darbe Mehrs in North America**
>
> *Arbab Rustom Guiv Darbe Mehr, New York, 1977*
> *Mehraban Guiv Darbe Mehr, Toronto, Ont., 1978*
> *Arbab Rustom Guiv Darbe Mehr, Chicago, 1983*
> *Arbab Rustom Guiv Darbe Mehr, Vancouver, BC, 1985*
> *Rustom Guiv Dar-e Mehr, Los Angeles, Calif., 1986*
> *North American Zoroastrian Center, Washington, D.C., 1990*
> *Zoroastrian Heritage and Cultural Center, Houston, Tex., 1996*

Religious Differences

Many tensions arise between traditional and liberal Zarathushtis because they have two very different views of their religion. The first group stresses the importance of the rituals and the limiting conditions of place that surround them. For them, the Vendidad—or the priestly code—with its ritual prescriptions, is very important. These prescriptions cannot be set aside and the traditional rituals cannot be adapted in any way.

Modern Zarathushtis, on the other hand, stress the ethical teachings of Zarathushtra as his central legacy. For them, rituals are not of the very essence of Zoroastrianism; and certainly their performance is, in practical terms, impossible outside the ancient sites of Iran and India. Liberal Zarathushtis, therefore, are willing to set aside the ritual practices. Some claim that it is impossible to carry out these ritual practices in modern circumstances. Others set the rituals aside simply because they see no reason to preserve them. For them, the Zoroastrian way of life— good thoughts, good words, and good deeds—is what is central to Zoroastrianism. For them, ritual-centered religion does not travel well around the world or in modern times. Modern Zarathushtis set their corresponding dedication to Zarathushtra's ethical teachings. They would rather meditate upon or dis-

A Haft Seen (traditional New Year's) table, decorated with items expressing family hopes for the coming year: adequate income, sweetness of life, fertility, etc.

cuss one of Zoroaster's Gathas than carry out a purification rite or even join in the chanting of a Gatha.

The question for Zarathushtis in today's world seems to be whether or not they can pick and choose any interpretation of the religion of Zarathushtra they want to follow. The conservative or traditionalist approach is to argue that one has to accept the whole message—the ethical code *and* the ritual of the Zoroastrian tradition. The liberal or modern interpretation sees the ethical message as the real essence of Zoroaster's religious contribution to the world of modern man. Some effort of accommodation seems necessary for the survival of Zoroastrianism, or a small group of dedicated religious people is going to wear itself out through serious family disputes.

The Question of Intermarriage

Among the most debated issues that splits traditionalist from liberal Zarathushtis is the question of intermarriage. The tradition among Zarathushtis was to marry other Zarathushtis as a way of strengthening and extending the religious and ethnic community. In the strongest traditional community, that of the Parsis in India, it is forbidden to marry someone of another religion. In their view, intermarriage begets religious compromises and discord. To marry someone of another faith is to abandon your own faith. For the Parsi, a person who intermarries is no longer considered a Zoroastrian. The children of such unions are also not considered "full" Zoroastrians; they are forbidden to take part in the highest religious rituals and may not enter the presence of the most sacred fires. For the traditionalist Zarathushtis, the child of a Zoroastrian father may be accepted for Navjote—the traditional ceremony of confirmation—in the Zoroastrian religion. A child of a Zoroastrian mother would not be accepted. For the liberal Zarathushtis of the diaspora, however, such a distinction between the treatment of children of Zarathushti fathers and mothers is unfair: the children should not be punished, they argue, so the children of either Zarathushti parent may be confirmed.

Such rules concerning membership seem quite reasonable when they are seen in terms of community survival. A small community has its best hope of survival in keeping to itself. This can be seen from the stories of other peoples. Many of the Jewish people lost their identity and their Biblical roots when the Assyrians captured them. The Assyrians had a policy of sending conquered people into different lands so that they would lose their identity through intermarriage. As a result, they would not be unified enough to rebel against their conquerors. A further consideration, however, is that in Persia and in India Zarathushtis had religiously solid and somewhat large Zoroastrian communities where it was quite possible to find a suitable Zoroastrian mate.

In the modern world, especially in the world of the diaspora where Zarathushtis are spread throughout many countries in small numbers, these conditions for suitable and favorable marriages with others of the same faith have disappeared. Certainly, Zarathushtis make all kinds of efforts to foster connections between young Zoroastrian men and women through associations and social events; even so, the odds seem stacked against finding someone with the same beliefs when so few exist who hold them. Permitting intermarriage seems most reasonable under these circumstances. However, the concerns that fostered prohibitions against intermarriage continue to return: if Zarathushtis intermarry, will they be able to preserve their religious identity?

Both traditionalist and liberal Zarathushtis recognize the dilemma they face, and though they are divided over how to resolve it, many in both groups have some understanding of the opposing view. They realize that on the one hand, marriage within the religion will be for the good of preserving the religion. They hold as a Zoroastrian ideal that one should be willing to sacrifice for the good of the community. However, given the conditions in the world of today when it is so difficult in a small religious community to find a suitable partner who shares one's faith, it might be worthwhile to look for other ways of attempting to preserve the faith even when marrying outside it.

Acceptance of Converts

Claiming to take Zoroaster's attitude as their model, traditionalist Zarathushtis argue that Zoroaster himself did not accept converts from outside religions. Neither, they argue, should his Zoroastrian followers. They contend that religion comes directly from God and that religious faith is different from explanations about religion. For traditionalists, it would be interference with God's will to convert someone to Zoroastrianism from the religion God gave them. Religion is not something someone can learn by studying. You cannot teach someone Zoroastrian religion because all religions are based on faith, and faith is God-given. Modern or liberal Zarathushtis disagree. For them, one can learn the basic message of Zarathushtra: good thoughts, good words, and good deeds. One can change one's way of life and live in accord with Zoroastrian teachings.

Certainly, a religion that has such small numbers, and numbers that are dispersed throughout the diaspora lands, runs the risk of reducing its numbers by limiting its adherents. The way to survival would be for traditionalist Zarathushtis to have large families, and traditional believers do, in fact, take this as their religious obligation. Yet, at least in the diaspora families who are Zoroastrian, the numbers of children are not large, and adherents are not pursuing marriage at an early age. Many want to finish their education and to begin careers before they start a family.

This situation leaves Zarathushtis with another dilemma. If they want to increase their numbers, they are limited by doing so in what seems the more practical way in today's world—by admitting converts. This might help to preserve the religious faith of someone who marries a person who is not a Zarathushti. The "outsider" might well become a strong follower of Zarathushtra's teachings and help raise his or her children as faithful and confirmed Zarathushtis. This approach might also temper concerns regarding intermarriage. Or should Zarathushtis adhere to the long, historical position that the traditionalists claim is the teaching of Zoroaster himself? To follow this position that would keep the religion unmixed would demand great sacrifices on the part of Zarathushtis; it also would not increase their numbers. No matter which road Zarathushtis choose, there is a risk. One road leads to a watering-down of their identity; the other risks eventual extinction.

Zoroastrianism's Success in the Modern World

Despite the difficulties it faces in preserving itself in the challenging modern context, the positive force of Zoroastrianism is undeniable. Both traditionalist and liberal Zarathushtis share the ethical way of the life of Zoroaster as a common inheritance. This guides them in their behavior, promotes hard work, and encourages educational excellence. These enrichments to human life defy time and place and put them in good stead in the many places Zarathushtis inhabit in this 21st-century world.

Another inheritance is found in Zoroastrians' social commitment. Zoroastrian communities stand by one another and support their members assiduously. They provide a network for getting jobs, offer practical assistance when members of the community need it, and offer moral support in times of trial and difficulties. The practical attitude of mind encouraged by

> ### ■ Zoroastrian Associations in North America
>
> *Zoroastrian Association of America, Chicago, USA, 1965**
> *Quebec, Canada, 1967*
> *British Columbia, Canada, 1968*
> *Ontario, Canada, 1971*
> *Greater New York, USA, 1973*
> *California, USA, 1974*
> *Metropolitan Chicago, USA, 1975*
> *Houston, USA, 1976*
> *Metropolitan Washington, (D.C.) USA, 1979*
> *Pennsylvania and New Jersey, USA, 1979*
> *California Zoroastrian Center, USA, 1980*
> *Zartoshti Anjuman of Northern California, USA, 1980*
> *Alberta, Canada, 1980*
> *Persian Zoroastrian Organization (Calif.), USA, 1981*
> *Pennsylvania, USA, 1982*
> *Greater Boston Area, USA, 1983*
> *Iranian Zoroastrian Association (N.Y.), USA, 1986*
> *Traditional Mazdayasni Zoroastrian Anjuman (Calif.), USA, 1980s*
> *North Texas, USA, 1989*
> *Kansas, USA, 1990*
> *Washington State, USA, 1990*
> *Arizona, USA, 1990*
> *Atlantic Canada, Canada, 1991*
> *Tampa Bay, Florida, USA, 2003*
>
> **year founded*

Zoroastrianism can be seen in all the associations that Zarathushtis create to help one another.

Having always been a minority, Zarathushtis are somewhat more at ease with small numbers than other groups might be. They are willing to go out on their own, moving to distant places to pursue job opportunities or education, trusting that they will find ways of linking up with their co-religionists. They have a penchant for establishing organizations and associations wherever they go. They face the modern world with a certain confidence. Zarathushtis have, as is evident from their many web pages, turned computers to their advantage. They have established networks that link co-religionists from all over the United States and Canada as well as among countries as diverse as Uzbekistan, Denmark, Australia, and Singapore.

■ *The Basic Daily Prayers of Zoroastrianism*

Ashem Vohu

Yatha ahu vairyo

Yenghe Hatam

Airyema Ishyo

The Kusti Prayers

■

The Contribution of Zoroastrianism to the World

Zoroastrians certainly communicate with one another. Yet because they do not seek converts, they do not advertise their religion to entice others to come join them. They do, however, set up networks of communication for themselves and, through them, we can find out something of their beliefs and history. In seeking to know more about Zoroaster, Zoroastrianism, and Zarathushtis, one almost senses that he or she is spying on a hidden world that has a life of its own. This religion is an important one, yet we hear so little about it.

As an ancient religion, one wonders whether its teachings have influenced any other ancient religions, especially the ones which, like Zoroastrianism, survive today. Many scholars have found that Zoroastrian teachings on the spirits of good and evil, heaven and hell, Satan, life after death, a Savior to come, the renewal of the world, and life everlasting have entered the worlds of Jewish, Christian, Islamic, and Buddhist belief. Still, these claims are usually not confirmed by any of these religions themselves. Zoroaster seems ignored by them or at least unknown to them. And so are Zarathushtis.

Zoroaster gained some recognition in the late 19th century when the philosopher Friedrich Nietzsche made him the main

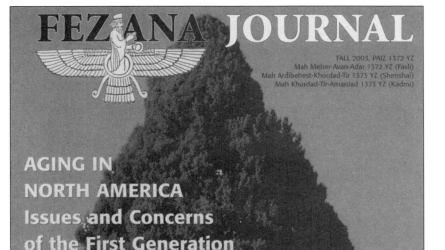

FEZANA JOURNAL

FALL 2003, PAIZ 1372 YZ
Mah Meher-Avan-Adar 1372 YZ (Fasli)
Mah Ardibehest-Khordad-Tir 1373 YZ (Shenshai)
Mah Khordad-Tir-Amardad 1373 YZ (Kadmi)

AGING IN
NORTH AMERICA
Issues and Concerns
of the First Generation

Also Inside:
Fezana AGM – Boston
NeXus 2003
Encourage New Business!
Healthy Living

PUBLICATION OF THE FEDERATION OF ZOROASTRIAN ASSOCIATIONS OF NORTH AMERICA

■ *Journals such as* Fezana *in North America and* Parsiana *in India provide the widely dispersed Zarathushti community with information about both their history and current affairs.*

character of his famous *Thus Spoke Zarathustra*. However, the work is more about Nietzsche than it is about Zarathushtra or Zoroaster; it provides a portrait of the anarchy that reigns in the author's soul as he surveys the battlefield on which good and evil fight their wars.

Zoroaster and Zoroastrianism have had much religious influence, but they have had it in a very quiet and unheralded way.

GLOSSARY

Achaemenids—The rulers of the Persian Empire from 552–330 B.C.E.

Afargan, afarganyu—A fire urn.

Afrin, afringen—A prayer invoking special blessings.

Agiary—The common name for a fire temple in India.

Ahriman—The Spirit of Evil (Pahlavi).

Ahunavaiti Gatha—Gathas 28–34.

Ahura Mazda—The supreme God of Zoroastrianism. Also known as Ohrmazd, Hormazd (Pahlavi).

Ameratat—A Beneficent Immortal; the spirit of Immortality and Joy after death.

Amesha Spentas—The Beneficent Immortals, aspects of Ahura Mazda.

Angra Mainyu—The Spirit of Evil (Avestan).

Armaity—*see* Spenta Armaity

Asha—Truth, righteousness.

Asha Vahista—A Beneficent Immortal; the Spirit of Truth and Righteousness.

Ashem Vohu—The basic prayer of Zoroastrianism.

Atash Adaran—A consecrated fire temple.

Atash Behram—A consecrated fire temple of the highest grade.

Atash Dadga—A fire temple.

Avesta—The Zoroastrian scripture.

Avestan—The ancient language in which Zoroastrian scripture is written.

Baj—The prayer before meals.

Boi—The ceremony for tending the sacred fire.

Bundahishn—The Zoroastrian story of creation.

Chinvat Bridge—The "Bridge of the Separator," where souls of the dead meet judgment.

Daena—Conscience; the spirit that meets a departed soul after death.

Daeva—A god of the old Iranian religion, considered evil.

Dakhma—The Tower of Silence; a structure used for disposing of the dead.

Darbe Mehr, Dar-e Meher—A fire temple.

Dastur—A Zoroastrian priest of India.

Dastur Dasturan—A Zoroastrian high priest.

Denkard—A summary of the contents of the Avesta; part of the Zand.

Dualism—The belief in two opposing forces, good and evil. Cosmic dualism is the belief that these two forces are part of the universe, and ethical dualism is the belief that these forces are within humankind.

Dughda—The mother of Zarathushtra.

Ervad—A Zoroastrian priest.

Faravahar (Farohar)—The winged symbol of Zoroastrianism.

Frashogard, Frashokereti—The renewal at the end of the world.

Fravashi—A Zoroastrian guardian spirit.

Gah, Geh—One of the five periods into which each day is divided for prayer; also, the prayer spoken at that time.

gahambar—One of six holy festivals of Zoroastrianism.

Gatha—One of seventeen hymns or psalms composed by Zarathushtra.

Gathic, Gathic Avestan—The language spoken by Zarathushtra.

Geh Sarna—The prayers for the dead.

Getig—The imperfect, physical world.

Great Avesta—The Avesta and related writings collected by the Sasanians.

Gujarati—A language of India, spoken by the Parsis.

Haoma—A plant used in ancient Iranian and later Zoroastrian rituals.

Haoma ritual—The principal ritual of the Yasna.

Haurvatat—A Beneficent Immortal; the spirit of Perfection and Well-being.

Hormazd—see Ahura Mazda

Humata, Hukhtra, Huvarshta—Good thoughts, good words, good deeds; the creed of Zoroastrianism.

Jashan—The ritual of memorial and thanksgiving.

Jizya—A tax levied on non-Muslims by Muslim rulers.

Kai, Kavi—An ancient Persian title meaning "king."

Khorda Avesta—The Zoroastrian book of daily prayers; part of the Avesta.

Khshathra Vairya—A Beneficent Immortal; the spirit of Ideal Authority or Dominion.

Kusti—The sacred cord received at the initiation ceremony, which is worn around the waist as a symbol of Zoroastrianism.

Lost Avesta—Sections of the Avesta destroyed by Arab and Muslim invasions. They were reproduced in the Zand from the oral tradition.

Magi—A priestly tribe from Media, in northwestern Iran.

Maidyoimanha (Medyomah)—Zarathushtra's cousin; the first person to accept Zoroastrianism.

Medes—People from Media, in northwestern Iran.

Menog—The perfect stage of the world before creation of the physical world.

Mithra—An ancient Iranian god. She later became a Zoroastrian angel of the Sun's light and of Truth; one of the judges of the soul.

Mobed—A Zoroastrian priest.

Mobed e Mobedan—A Zoroastrian high priest.

Navjote—The Zoroastrian initiation ceremony.

NoRoz—The Zoroastrian New Year, a holy feast day.

Nyayesh—Zoroastrian prayers from the Avesta.

Ohrmazd—see Ahura Mazda

Pahlavi—The Middle Persian language, spoken by the Sasanians; the language of Avesta commentary.

Panchayat—The governing body of Parsis in India.

Parsi—A Zoroastrian of India.

Parthian dynasty—The Zoroastrian rulers (250 B.C.E.–226 C.E.) who began a collection of the Avesta.

Patet—The prayer of repentance.

Qajar dynasty—The Muslim dynasty that ruled Iran until 1925.

Rashnu—The spirit of Justice; one of the judges of the soul.

Rivyats—Letters from Parsis to Zoroastrian priests of Iran, from the fourteenth to the sixteenth centuries.

Sagid—The "Gaze by the dog" death ritual.

Sasanian (Sasanid) dynasty—The dynasty (226–651 C.E.) that standardized Zoroastrian ritual and collected the Avesta.

Saoshyant—The Savior to come.

Seleucid empire—The empire established by Greek rulers after the death of Alexander.

Spenta Armaity—A Beneficent Immortal; the Spirit of Love and Devotion.

Spenta Mainyu—The holy Spirit of Truth; an aspect of Ahura Mazda.

Spenta Mainyu Gatha—Gathas 47–50.

Sraosha—The angel of obedience; one of the judges of the soul.

Sudreh—The sacred undergarment received at the initiation ceremony.

Ustavaiti Gatha—Gathas 43–46.

Vahisto Ishti Gatha—Gatha 53.

Vendidad—The section of the Avesta containing the priestly code.

Vishtaspa—A legendary king; an early follower of Zarathushtra.

Visperad—The section of the Avesta with liturgy for the holy days.

Vohu Khshathra Gatha—Gatha 51.

Vohu Mana—A Beneficent Immortal; the Spirit of the Good Mind.

Yashts—A section of the Avesta containing hymns to saints and angels.

Yasna—The first section of the Avesta, containing the basic liturgy and the Gathas.

Yasna Haptanhaiti—A liturgy believed to have been composed by Zarathushtra.

Yazatas—Zoroastrian angels and holy beings.

Young Avesta—The portion of the Avesta written in the later form of Avestan.

Young Avestan—The language that replaced Gathic Avestan.

Zand (Zend)—Commentary and translations of the Avesta, written in Pahlavi.

Zarathushti—A Zoroastrian.

Zarathushti Din—The Zoroastrian religion.

Zarathushtra—The Prophet of the Zoroastrian religion.

Zartoshti—An Iranian Zoroastrian.

Zoroaster—Zarathushtra (Greek).

CHAPTER NOTES

page 17	"Then thus spake Ahura Mazda. . . ."
pages 17–18	"And thus spoke Ahura Mazda. . . ."
pages 21–22	"Verily, I have chosen him. . . ."
pages 49–50	"In humble adoration, . . ."
page 51	"In the beginning . . ."
page 51	"What are thy commandments? . . ."
page 52	"This I ask Thee. . . ."
page 53	"Whoso shuns the evil-liars . . ."
pages 53–54	"He, who following Truth, . . ." Dinshaw J. Irani, *Understanding the Gathas: The Hymns of Zarathushtra.*
page 70	Irani, *Understanding the Gathas*
page 71	"O Ahura Mazda, we praise Thee. . . ." The Zoroastrian Society of Greater New York, *The Good Life.*
page 77	Irani, *Understanding the Gathas*

FOR FURTHER READING

Choksy, Jamsheed. *Evil, Good and Gender: Facets of the Feminine in Zoroastrian Religious History.* New York: Peter Lang, 2002.

Clark, Peter. *Zoroastrianism: An Introduction to an Ancient Faith.* Brighton, Eng. and Portland, Oreg.: Sussex Academic Press, 1999.

Irani, Dinshaw. *Understanding the Gathas.* Wommelsdorf, Pa.: Ahura Publishers, Inc., 1994.

Kellens, Jean. *Essays on Zarathustra and Zoroastrianism.* Costa Mesa, Calif.: Mazda Publishers, 2000.

Nanavutty, Pillo. *The Gathas of Zarathushtra: Hymns in Praise of Wisdom.* Ahmedabad, India: Mapin Publishing, 1999.

Rivetna, Roshan, ed. *The Legacy of Zarathushtra.* Hinsdale, Ill.: Federation of Zoroastrianism Associations of North America, 2002.

Writer, Rashna. *Contemporary Zoroastrians: An Unconstructed Nation.* Lanham, Md.: University Press of America, 1994.

INDEX

Achaemenids 36–39
Afargan, afarganyu 16
Afrin, afringan prayer 99
Afterlife 18, 19, 70–71, 72, 89
Agiary 17
Ahriman. *see* Angra Mainyu
Ahunavaiti Gatha. *see* Avesta, Gathas
Ahura Mazda (one God), and
   Amesha Spentas 78–79; and free
   will 10, 12; and Gathas 66–67,
   68–69, 71; names of 75; qualities of
   6, 10, 18–19; and sacred fire 15–16;
   and Zarathushtra 9–10, 25, 26–27,
   28, 34; worship of 53
Ahura Mazda Khodae 88
Airyema Ishyo 101
Alexander the Great 39, 64
Ameratat. *see* Philosophy and ethics
Amesha Spentas 11–12, 26, 36, 69–71,
   78–79, 81, 83, 85, 95, 96
Angelic beings. *see* Beneficent
   Immortals, Yazatas
Angra Mainyu, (evil force) 10, 13, 19,
   28, 36, 39, 74, 85–86, 88
Animals, role of 25, 27
Anquetil-Duperon, Abraham 65
Ardashir 41–42
Armaity. *see* Philosophy and ethics;
   Spenta Armaity
Asha (path of truth) 9, 10, 78, 80–81,
   85–86. *see also* Philosophy and
   ethics
Asha Vahista 12
Ashem Vohu 80, 99
Associations 111, 118
Atash Adaran 17
Atash Behram 17, 52–53, 92, 95
Atash Dadga 17
Avesta 6, 15, 25, 26, 32, 40–41, 44;
   Ahunavaiti 67–69; Bundahishn
   76–77; contents of 65–66; destruc-
   tion by Alexander 64; fragments of
   76; Gathas 66–67; history of 62–65;
   importance of 62, 77; minor texts
   74–76; oral tradition 63–64; Pahlavi
   Zand 76; Spenta Mainyu 71–72;
   understanding 72–73; Ustavaiti
   69–71; Vahisto Ishti 72; Vendidad
   74; Visperad 65, 73, 80; Vohu
   Khshathra 72; Yashts 65, 73–74;

Yasna 65, 66, 90; and Zarathushtra
   62, 65, 66
Avestan language. *see* Gathic, Gathic
   Avestan; Young Avestan
Ayathrima. *see* Rituals and rites of
   passage, High Holy Days

Bactria 34
Balkh 31, 34
Beneficent Immortal (archangels) 27,
   36, 88
Boi 17
Buddhism 43
Bukhara 44
Bundahishn. *see* Avesta, Bundahishn
Bridge of the Separator. *see* Chinvat
   Bridge
British Raj 55

Calendar. *see* Zoroastrian calendars
Chinvat Bridge 73, 105
Christianity 43
Community 8–9
Comparison with other religions 18
Conservative followers 113, 114, 116
Conscience 12–13
Consciousness 10
Cosmic dualism 85. *see also*
   Philosophy and ethics, dualism
Creation 9, 28, 36, 42, 76–77, 85, 86
Creed 10–11, 66
Cyrus the Great 19, 36–37, 41

Daena 105
Daitya River 26
Dakhma 55, 102. *see also* Rituals and
   rites of passage, Towers of Silence
Darbe Mehr (Dar-e Meher) 17, 111,
   113
Darius 38
Dastur (priest). *see* Rituals and rites of
   passage, priesthood
Dastur Dasturan (high priest). *see*
   Rituals and rites of passage, priest-
   hood
Death 18, 19, 28, 55
Denkard. see Avesta, Pahlavi Zand
Deities, names of 64
Din No Kalmo 100
Diu community 48, 51

Divine essence 13
Dualism. *see* Philosophy and ethics
Dughda 23, 24–25

Ervad. *see* Rituals and rites of passage
Ethics. *see* Philosophy and ethics
Ethical dualism 85. *see also*
   Philosophy and ethics, dualism

Faravahar (Farohar) symbol 8–9, 38
Fasli calendar. *see* Zoroastrian calendars
Festivals. *see* High Holy Days and rituals
Fezana Journal 120
Fire, and afterlife 28; *afarghan* 93; ceremonies 92–93; sacred 15–16, 48, 53,
   54, 92; temples 17–18, 65, 79, 80, 92.
   see also Rituals and rites of passage
Frashaoshtra 72
Frashogard (Frashokereti) 13, 89, 96
Fravashi 9, 12–13, 73, 89
Free will 10, 12, 19, 82
Future of Zoroastrianism 112–113;
   contributions to the world 119–120;
   converts 110, 116–117; intermarriage 110, 114–116; modern times
   117–119; religious differences
   113–114; threats to survival
   110–112; youth 110–112. *see also*
   History, modern life

Gabar 45
Gah (Geh). *see* Avesta; minor texts
Gahambar. see Rituals and rites of pas-
   sage, High Holy Days
Gathas (psalms) 9, 13, 22, 23, 31,
   66–67
Gathic (Gathic Avestan) 22, 42, 62, 66,
   72
Gayomart. *see* Avesta, Bundahishn
Geh Sarna ceremony 103
Getig world. *see* Philosophy and
   ethics
Gandhi, Prime Minister Rajiv 60
Gnosticism 43
Good and Evil, and
   Faravahar/Farohar symbol 9; final
   battle 88–89; question of 18–19; and
   Spirits 10, 11–12; struggle between

9, 10, 11–12, 14, 28, 36, 68, 78, 81–82, 86–87
Good Mind. *see* Vohu Mana
Good thoughts, words, and deeds 9, 11, 29, 68, 77, 78, 81–82, 100
Great Avesta 64
Guardian spirits 9, 12, 25
Gumeisn world. *see* Philosophy and ethics
Gujarati. *see* India, settlement in Gujarat, Surat, and Navsari

Hamaspathmaedaya, Muktad. *see* Rituals and rites of passage, High Holy Days
Haoma plant 25, 35, 73; ritual 35, 90
Hataria, Manekji 45–46
Haurvatat. *see* Amesha Spentas; Philosophy and ethics
History of Zoroastrianism, and Achaemenid Empire 36–39; Afghani invasion 45; and Greeks 32, 39–40, 65; and early Zoroastrianism 34–35; gathering the Avesta 42–43; and growth of and changes to Zoroastrianism 35–36; inscriptions from reign of Cyrus and Darius 77; and Judaism 37; and Magi 35–36, 38; modern Iran 46–47; Muslim conquest 43–45, 92; nineteenth century 45–46; official state religion 42–43; and Parthians 40–41; and Qajar invasian 45; and Sasanians 41–43; settlement in India 45
Holy Days, High 8, 14, 23, 65, 73, 95–97
Hormazd. *see* Ahura Mazda
Hormazd Yasht. *see* Avesta, Yashts
Hormuz community 48, 50–51
Household shrine 20, 21
Humata, Hukhta, Huvarshta 9, 11
Hvovi 31

India and Zoroastrianism 8, 45; assimilation of social customs 54–55; Atash Bahram in Udwada 52; battle at Sanjan 54; Bombay 49, 50, 51, 55, 87; British rule 53–58; caste system 54; contributions of Parsis 57; life in 53–54; modern life 58–61; Muslim invaders 54, 76; Parsi migration 50–51, 54, 60–61; Parsi Rivyats 54–55; partitionment 60; prosperity 56–57, 58; rioting 57; settlement in Gujarat, Surat, and Navsari 48, 51
Iran 8, 15, 24, 32, 45–47
Isaiah 37
Isfahan 45
Isfendiyad 30
Islam 44–45, 48
Islamic Republic 47

Jadi Rana 53
Jamaspa Hvogva 30, 31, 35, 72
Jashan ceremony. *see* Rituals and rites of passage
Jizya 45

Kai Vishtaspa 29–30, 34, 68
Khomeinei, Ayatollah Ruhollah 47, 108
Khorasan Mountain community 48, 50–51
Khorda Avesta. *see* Avesta; minor texts
Khshathra Vairya. *see* Amesah Spentas; Philosophy and ethics
Kirman 45, 55
Kusti 99–100
Kusti prayers 98

"Lament of the Cow, The" 67–68
Language of Zoroastrianism 42, 54–55, 72–73
Liberal followers 113–114, 116
Literature 55. *see also* Avesta
Lost Avesta 65

Magi 26, 35–36, 38
Maidhyairya. *see* Rituals and rites of passage, High Holy Days
Maidhyoimanha (Medyomah) 29, 72
Maidhyoishema. *see* Rituals and rites of passage, High Holy Days
Maidhyoizaremaya. *see* Rituals and rites of passage, High Holy Days
Mainyu. *see* Philosophy and ethics, dualism
Mani and Manichaeism 43
Mazdak 43
Mazdayazni religion 77
Mehta, Zubin 58–59
Menog. *see* Philosophy and ethics
Merv 44
Migrations. *see* History; India
Mithra 40, 73, 99, 105
Mithridates I and II 40
Mobed. *see* Rituals and rites of passage, priesthood
Mobed e Mobedan. *see* Rituals and rites of passage, priesthood
Morality 55, 58, 69–70, 77, 81, 83; importance of 78
Muslims 60. *see also* History

Nahan 100
Navjote ceremony 81, 82, 94, 95
Nirang 100, 106
NoRoz 14, 97. *see also* Rituals and rites of passage, High Holy Days
Nyayesh. *see* Avesta, minor texts

Ohramazd 13, 42. *see also* Ahura Mazda
Origins 6, 8

Pahlavi language 42, 44, 54–55, 65, 75
Pahlavi, Shah Mohammed Reza 47
Pahlavi, Shah Reza 46
Paitshahya. *see* Rituals and rites of passage, High Holy Days
Pakistan 60
Panchayat 54
Parsi 8, 45, 53; exclusivity and definition 61
Parthian dynasty 40–41, 64
Patet prayer 100, 106
Persecution 44–45, 47, 48, 92
Persepolis 8, 33, 34, 38, 64
Persia 8, 22, 26, 30, 31; climate 34; history of 32–47, 64–65; origins of people 32–33; Persian gulf 51; tribal customs 34
Philosophy and ethics, and Amesha Spentas 78–79; Armaity 83; Asha, the Path of Truth 80–81; dualism 83–86; Frashogart 89; Good Mind The, 81–82; Haurvatat and

Ameratat 12, 83; Khshathra Vairya: Just Dominion 9, 12, 83; Menot, Getig, and Gumeisn worlds 86–88; and other religions 18. *see also* Good and Evil; Morality
Pouruchista 31, 72
Pourushasp 23–25
Prayer 10, 14, 17, 44, 50, 66–67, 74–75, 88, 98, 119
Priestly code. *see* Avesta, Vendidad

Qadmi (Kadmi) calendar. *see* Zoroastrian calendars
Qajar dynasty 45–46
Qutaiba ibn Muslim 44

Rashnu 73, 105
Revelation 9–10
Rituals and rites of passage 14–16, 35, 74; Boi-Machi Ceremony 92–93; fire 90, 92; funerals 103; High Holy Days 14, 93, 95–97; Jashan: Thanksgiving and Memorial 91, 92, 98–99; Navjote 99–101, 110; prayers for the dead 105–106; priesthood 7, 8, 16, 53, 55, 63–64, 94–95; threats to survival 112; towers of silence 102, 103–105; weddings 101–102. *see also* Holy Days, High
Rivyats. *see* India and Zoroastrianism

Sagid ceremony 103
Salvation 18, 72, 82
Saoshyant 89
Sasanian (Sasanid) dynasty 41–43, 64
Savior. *see* Saoshyant
Scripture. *see* Avesta
Seleucid Empire 39–40
Shapur I 42
Shenshai calendar. *see* Zoroastrian calendars

Spenta Armaity (Generosity and Love). *see* Amesha Spentas, Spenta Armaity
Spenta Mainyu 10, 28, 71–72, 85–86
Spenta Mainyu Gatha. *see* Avesta, Gathas
Spirit of Truth. *see* Avesta, Spenta Mainyu
Spirits 73. *see also* Beneficent Immortal
Spitama clan 23
Sraosha 73, 105
Srishok 92
Sudreh 99
Sudre-Pushti. *see* Rituals and rites of passage, Navjote
Symbol (Faravahar), meaning of 9; picture 8

Tata, Jehangir Ratan D. 57
Temples 17–18. *see also* Atash Behram, Atash Adaran, Atash Dadga
Temptation 14, 19

Udwada, India 52
Ustavaiti Gatha. *see* Avesta, Gathas

Vahisto Ishti Gatha. *see* Avesta, Gathas
Valerian 42
Vendidad. *see* Avesta, Vendidad
Vishtaspa 72
Visperad. *see* Avesta, Visperad
Vohu Khshathra Gatha. *see* Avesta, Gathas
Vohu Mana. *see* Amesha Spentas

Women's role 19, 29, 56–57
Worship 14–15, 53, 65–66

Xerxes 38–39

Yashts 65. *see also* Avesta, Yashts
Yasna. *see* Avesta, Visperdad
Yasna Haptanhaiti. *see* Avesta, Yasna
Yazatas 65–66, 73
Yazd 45, 55
Yazdegard III 43–44, 48
Young Avestan 62, 66, 73

Zand (Zend) 43, 65. *see also* Avesta, Pahlavi Zand
Zarathushti 77, 78, 82, 110, 112, 117
Zarathushti Din. *see* Zoroastrianism
Zarathushtra 6, 17; birthday celebration 23; death of 31; early ministry and converts 26–27, 28–30, 34–35; later life 30–31; message of reform 27–29; miraculous birth 24–25; oral tradition 20; ordination by Ahura Mazda 26–27; probable origins 20, 22–23; quest for truth 26; representations of 21–23; vision 27; writing 20, 21, 22, 66–67
Zartoshti. *see* Zoroastrianism
Zoroaster. *see* Zarathushtra
Zoroastrian calendars 93
Zoroastrianism, and afterlife 18, 19, 44; in Avesta 62–77; basic principles of 9–11, 66–67; conquered by Islam 44–45; creed or goals of 10–11, 14; dispersal of Persian believers 44–45, 108; importance of doing good 14; law 76; and other religions 18, 44; origins 6; purified by Sasanids 42; size and location of community 8–9; and restoration of the world 13–14; and the soul 12–13; spread of 26; standardization 42–43; successes in the modern world 117–119